Adventure on Joyland Road
and Other Stories of Love and Grief

Lisa Rosenberg, PhD, RN

Potter's Wheel Publishing House
Minneapolis

Potter's Wheel Publishing House
Minneapolis

*Adventure on Joyland Road
and Other Stories of Love and Grief*
by Lisa Rosenberg, PhD, RN

Published by POTTER'S WHEEL PUBLISHING HOUSE
MINNEAPOLIS, MN 55378

www.POTTERSWHEELPUBLISHING.com

© 2025 Lisa Rosenberg

All rights reserved. No part of this publication may be reproduced, stored in a retrieval system, or transmitted, in any form or in any means—by electronic, mechanical, photocopying, recording or otherwise—without prior written permission, except as permitted by U.S. copyright law.

For permissions contact:
info@POTTERSWHEELPUBLISHING.com

ISBN: 978-1-950399-22-2

LCCN: 2024953122

Praise for Adventure on Joyland Road

Dr. Rosenberg is a gifted writer and storyteller. Adventure on Joyland Road is marvelous, straightforward, funny, and honest, written with great joy and great sadness but so much wisdom. Even as a seasoned mental health professional, I came to understand more fully that grief is a process, not a pathology. The many important lessons in Dr. Rosenberg's work need to be shared, along with the many truths that are rarely put into words. This is truly a beautiful book.

Karen Pierce, M.D.
Distinguished Fellow of the American Psychiatric Association and the American Academy of Child and Adolescent Psychiatry

The sudden, unexpected death of a loved one confronts a survivor with unanswerable questions about life's goodness and fairness, and there are very few resources available to help a survivor regain trust in our world. This is why Dr. Lisa Rosenberg's book, *Adventure on Joyland Road*, is essential reading for anyone who suddenly lost a loved one or for their family and friends. Dr. Rosenberg's passionate writing draws us into the moment she lost her beloved husband and invites us to accompany her on her journey to healing and wholeness. Her story inspires others to find their way to begin living again.

Rabbi Robert S. Feinberg
Chaplain, U.S. Navy (retired)

Grieving the loss of a loved one is a deeply personal journey, one for which few of us are prepared. In this beautifully written memoir, Dr. Lisa Rosenberg shares her insights on learning to live with profound loss and the path she has forged to find peace with a new normal through reflection, humor, and self-compassion. Those who have experienced personal loss will find enormous comfort in this book, knowing that our lives are richer because of the people we've loved.

Deborah Gross, DNSc, RN, FAAN
Leonard and Helen Stulman Endowed Professor in Mental Health & Psychiatric Nursing Johns Hopkins School of Nursing

Table of Contents

Preface 1

Section 1: Of Stories, Sweet and Bittersweet 5

    How We Met and the Seven Words 7

    Becoming Who We Are 16

    When Everything Changed in an Instant 30

Section 2: What Does Grief Feel Like? 41

    Grief Makes You Weary 43

    A Visit from Guilt 47

    "I Am Shattered" 50

    Dancing with Grief 53

    Aren't I Supposed to Be Feeling Better by Now? 58

    Who Am I? 62

Section 3: Memories 65

    Walking the Knife's Edge of Memory 67

    The Small Moments 75

    A Thousand Cuts 78

    The Meaning of Stuff 80

Section 4: Love and Grief 87

    Weaving the Tapestry of Love 89

    The Space Where Love Existed 94

    Groundhog Day 96

    My Lodestar 101

    Woodstock 104

    The Unseen Presence 108

    May 20 111

Section 5: Sometimes There Are No Answers 117

    Tears Without Warning 119

    Going to the Airport Is a Killer 123

    Decisions, Decisions, Decisions 126

    Expect the Unexpected 128

    Reinventing Yourself 131

    Everything's Okay Until It's Not 134

Section 6: Strategies to Cope 139

    You Have to Own Your Life, No One Else Can 141

    Accomplish Something Small Every Day 146

    Say Yes When It Feels Right 149

    The Kindness of Others and Compassionate Listening 153

    The Good, Bad, and Trivial Moments 157

    The Virtue of Humor 164

    The Enchantment of Nature 173

    The Unexpected Silence 181

    I Can Do Anything If I Want To (Within Reason) 184

    The Power of Friends and Family 190

    The X Factor 199

Section 7: Philosophical Ponderings 205

    The Necessity of Distraction 207

    Hoping Against Reality 209

    The Crucible of Loss 213

    The Calm 216

    The Grace of Gratitude 218

    I Need a Sign 222

    The Legacy They Leave 228

Reflections on Elisabeth Kübler-Ross and the Stages of Grief 236
Wait for Me 246
This Is Not Creepy 253
Adventure on Joyland Road 255

Epilogue 258
Notes 261
Acknowledgments 265

"There is nothing more whole than a broken heart."
Rabbi Menachem Mendel of Kotzk (1787–1859)

"Amor mi mosse, che mi fa parlare"—translated as
"Love has moved me, and makes me speak."
Dante Alighieri from La Commedia (The Divine Comedy),
completed in 1321.

To Jeff
In every possible way

Preface

    This isn't the book I intended to write. During my 30 years as a college professor, a slice of my academic life was devoted to writing journal articles—mostly for the benefit of my colleagues—on my research, interesting case studies, or innovative programs I developed. Because I enjoyed writing during my academic career, I thought I'd continue after retirement. However, I had yet to take the first step since leaving work. And then, suddenly, my husband of almost 30 years passed away. One day he was moving, breathing, laughing, and saying goodnight to me. The next morning, he was gone—my loving, funny Jeff.

    I was devastated; our world shattered as quickly as midnight lightning silently strikes a steadfast but vulnerable oak, felling it to the forest floor. I started making notes within a month of Jeff's passing—thoughts important to remember as I tried to make sense of this tragic event and navigate through it. I'd never done anything like that before, but I was at such a loss, unsure how to move forward. If a thought struck an emotional chord, it was worth noting. Perhaps it would buoy my resolve and give me the strength to surface from my grief and breathe again.

    Beyond the sheer emotional impact of my husband's death, the change in everyday life after losing a loved one—particularly when it's sudden—is stunning. The first 18 months after your loved one dies are unimaginably hard. Early on, the visceral emotionality of grief leaves one in pure survival mode. Experiences are now filtered through a different lens, and the texture of time is altered. Feelings of loss and grief don't simply disappear after a year and a half, but unexpected emotions that catch you off guard tend to lessen over time. I'm still on a learning curve, but I experience fewer thunderbolts to the chest knocking me off my feet.

During those first 18 months after Jeff's death, I began to mindfully examine the smaller moments of my life and what I was experiencing. What resulted was a profoundly emotional and revealing journey in which larger lessons emerged. What I've written in the following pages is my truth, the way I sought to make meaning of my grief. Some of these reflections may resonate with you.

There's an inherent paradox in trying to describe the lived experience of grief. One's encounter with grief feels so unique and profound—how could anyone else possibly comprehend the depth and breadth of losing your precious love? Yet, an unrestrained and focused examination of this lived experience can be raw and revelatory, exposing the ferocity of life to which we bore witness.

In his book, *The Lived Experience*, van Manen wrote that a focused introspection encourages us to be attentive and aware of the details and seemingly trivial aspects of our daily lives. "It makes us thoughtfully aware of the consequential in the inconsequential, the significance in the taken-for-granted." This thoughtful awareness can foster a deeper understanding of the lived experience of grief. When the stories of our loss are told with honest reflection, they become compelling—they help us uncover the meaning of our experiences in the world. Revealing personal insights and truths is a door for others to walk through, allowing them to see their experiences as shared and connected with someone else. Reading a deft description of an experience you believed was yours alone may bring comfort, knowing someone else truly "gets it." What you, the reader, take from it is distinctive to you. But still, there's no "get-out-of-grief free" card. As far as I can tell, you don't walk away from grief but find a way to walk with it.

Throughout our lives, as we grow up and grow old in a culturally complex society, we develop a range of ways to think about and perceive experiences. But that range is finite. While the pain of the loss of someone you love feels so deeply personal and indescribable, those who belong to this unsolicited club share more with other survivors than they first might realize. While you don't want people, especially those you care about, to go through grief that feels so exquisitely hard to bear, they inevitably will if they have loved deeply.

The first notes I wrote to myself were strictly my thoughts and feelings related to grieving and how I could cope with what had happened. But as I continued to write and give voice to my reflections, I began to write about love. You don't write about profound grief without having profoundly loved, as the two travel hand-in-hand. C.S. Lewis, the British scholar and theologian, wrote in *A Grief Observed*, "If, as I can't help suspecting, the dead also feel the pains of separation, then for both lovers, and for all pairs of lovers without exception, bereavement is a universal and integral part of our experience of love."

Though this book is, first and foremost, a memoir, my understanding of the grief process is filtered through my personal and academic identities—they are inextricably intertwined. In the following pages, I share many stories, about my husband, myself, and our relationship, interwoven with knowledge, research, humor, and wisdom to create a broader context for understanding bereavement in the first 18 months.

This book* contains seven themed sections, each featuring stories that explore how these themes take shape. It follows a loose chronology, as there is no orderly narrative arc to the experience of profound grief. It doesn't follow a neat, linear path—where you finish one stage and move on to the next. Several chapters in the book have

Adventure on Joyland Road

their own chronology, as one's perceptions change over 18 months. For example, in the chapter "A Visit from Guilt," my experience of guilt shifted over time, and it was important to say how that happened. There's a saying that form follows function. In this case, form follows experience. Grief is a collection of wavy, dotted lines, crossing over and intersecting with one another. One day, you're functioning well; the next, you're a puddle of tears. If your experience of loving someone had all the highs and lows of what life puts in front of you, why wouldn't grief feel the same? Both grief and love are messy and surprising.

For any reader who has loved someone deeply and lost that person, there is something here for you. I urge you to tell your own stories of love and loss, to articulate them so you can hear yourself think. Everyone's journey is different, and the meaning you discover is uniquely yours. Finding meaning is how you move forward, allowing you to make some peace with the immutable.

---

* All the individuals mentioned in this book are real. Most of their names have been changed to respect their privacy.

Section 1:
Of Stories, Sweet and Bittersweet

It's important to understand how Jeff and I found each other, what shaped his identity, and how he was gone in an instant. By understanding our story—and, in turn, telling your own or your loved one's—you create context for yourself and others to grasp the magnitude of your grief; it becomes more knowable. Making meaning of what happened, this tragic and uncontrollable tide you would have given anything to prevent, begins with looking at how deeply you loved.

In his memoir, All Over but the Shoutin'*, Rick Bragg wrote about the death of his beloved grandmother, "Maybe, if I tell it right, she will live again on these pages, that all the things she could have shared about who we are, who I am, will not be so badly missed. I like to believe that." Everyone's story of how they got to this place, which often defies description or measure, is worth telling. It's the solid foundation upon which your grief rests.*

How We Met and the Seven Words

My divorce from my first husband, Ben, became official in January 1992. Ben and I married when I was 20—not recommended—and divorced 17 years later. Once the divorce was final, I started to date a little but had no real sense of what the future might hold. Though I was a dog lover, I'd never owned one, so I got Mike from the local shelter to keep me company. In retrospect, I'm not sure I was doing the dog any favors.

In March of 1992, I decided to join my best friend and her family on a trip to Disney World. It was a good, safe way to get away and be with friends. However, on my return trip home, on a Saturday, I began to feel ill. By the time I arrived at O'Hare Airport in Chicago, I was fully engulfed by a terrible virus: sore throat, cough, and a nasty head cold. As I labored to the baggage claim, I saw my sister in the airport waiting for me. That was odd. My parents had said they would pick me up—this was before ride-hailing services were a thing, when family or friends would actually drive to the airport to retrieve you. I asked my sister why she was there instead of my parents. She exclaimed hastily, "Mom had a little stroke."

Being a nurse, I was alarmed and wary of just how little this stroke might be. She said my mother was in the hospital and then described what had occurred. I called my dad as soon as I got home. He confirmed my mother was stable, and I could see her the next day.

When I got home, a man I didn't know had left a message on my answering machine. The husband of someone I worked with had given my name and number to a friend. This mystery man was calling to talk with me and, presumably, ask me out on a blind date. Because he had no idea I was out of town for a week, he called three times, leaving a message each time. Why call three times? He said he liked the sound of my voice on the answering machine.

But it was Jeff who had the memorable voice. It was deep and soothing, reminiscent of the singer, Barry White. I found it intriguing. His message said he'd call back in a couple of days. Over the 30 years that followed, Jeff never lost the deep, resonant timbre of his voice. It was like a warm blanket enveloping you, keeping you sheltered and safe from a swirling storm outside.

The following day, Sunday, I was sick as a dog and sounded like one; my voice was no better than a howling rasp. That day I did receive a call, but not from Jeff, who was still a mystery man to me. It was Ben, my ex-husband, telling me he had just gotten married. I did not necessarily see this coming, and it felt as if whatever semi-solid ground I was standing on was falling away beneath my feet. Short though it was, I cannot recall the rest of the conversation with Ben, as any sense of belonging to my previous life was being irrevocably crushed.

Jeff called on Monday. I was thrilled, but I was so ill I could barely speak. I was hoping my gravelly voice was reminiscent of Lauren Bacall but feared it sounded more like a sick bloodhound. We chit-chatted about the two people we knew, Phillip and Linda, who orchestrated the blind date. Phillip, a physician, had an office next to Jeff. His wife, Linda, was my colleague in the nursing college where I worked, and she made the blind date connection. Jeff, as it turned out, was a child psychiatrist. He and I were both healthcare providers, and my specialty just happened to be psychiatric nursing—this seemed promising. Jeff was separated from his wife and in the process of getting a divorce. He had two adolescent children, and I was childless. At the time, I had no idea of the pertinence of these last facts.

After about twenty minutes of conversation, my throat was so sore I could barely speak. I painfully uttered, "Look, can we talk again in a couple of days? I have this bad cold, my mother is in the hospital with a stroke, and my ex-husband called yesterday to tell me he just got married." In retrospect, this flagrant sharing did not seem like a good move to ensure a call-back for a blind date. I worked at a large academic medical center that employed 10,000 people, but no one there seemed the least bit interested in pursuing me. Even worse, I didn't know Jeff's friends had already pressed 10 phone numbers into his hand of available women anxious to meet him. I wasn't thinking clearly that day so, there it was, an unbridled transparency of my woes.

Jeff did call back in two days, and I was feeling a bit better. He said he felt bad for me based on the recent events I described and wanted to take me to dinner. He named three very lovely fine dining establishments in Chicago: The Everest Room, The 95th in the Hancock Building, and the original Yoshi's restaurant (they opened Yoshi's Café several years later). I was surprised by these upscale options, but certainly not displeased. I chose Yoshi's as it was close to the hospital where my mother was a patient. I asked Jeff how I would know him at the restaurant, which he correctly perceived to be a thinly veiled attempt to ask, "And what do you look like?" Without missing a beat he said, "I'm a bald, middle-aged Jewish psychiatrist who drives a SAAB." Knowing I'd been caught in my superficial quest for information, I responded enthusiastically, "I drive a SAAB, too!"

I visited my mom on the day of our date and then drove from the hospital to Yoshi's. I became more apprehensive as I approached the restaurant. Was this going to be the rest of my life, meeting bald, middle-aged, Jewish men at nice restaurants? As I reached the front of the restaurant, Jeff was getting out of his SAAB—a bald, middle-aged man, just as he had described himself. I panicked, drove around the block to calm myself, and then finally parked my car.

Adventure on Joyland Road

I walked into the restaurant and Jeff was seated in a booth, patiently waiting for me. He was wearing a 3-piece gray suit and had six pink roses sitting next to him. I was thrown off by the suit; I wasn't expecting the formality. The pink roses were a lovely touch. We sat at that booth for the next four hours and talked about our lives (tattered and frayed at the moment), our jobs, interests, where we grew up—all the typical first date conversation and more.

Jeff kissed me when we left the restaurant and said he would like to see me again. I replied, "Okay," but, in my head, I wasn't sure. I'd never met anyone like him—mature, perceptive, and scrupulously honest—a man completely comfortable in his own skin. And he wanted to know exactly who I was, too. I didn't fully appreciate at the time, probably because I was too nervous, that I was on a date with a very bright and gifted psychiatrist. He assessed I was worth a second date, but I was still wavering.

It wasn't as if I had created a list of criteria a man had to meet for me to go out with him. It's great to have things in common with someone, but I didn't have a checklist of must-haves—for example, likes watching sports (he did), plays golf (he didn't), or in a healthcare profession (he just happened to be). In retrospect, when I think back with the hindsight of who I fell in love with and married, I believe I did have a list of non-negotiable characteristics: *nice, smart, and funny*. A short list for sure, but all elements are required. I highly recommend these qualities should you find yourself in a similar situation.

Jeff called in a day or two, and we set up another date for two weeks later. He had visitation with his children the upcoming weekend so we needed to wait until then. This gave me plenty of time to decide whether I wanted to go on Date Two. I vacillated but finally decided, "Why not give it a try?" We don't have to go on Date 3 if it doesn't click. I lived 40 miles away from Jeff, truly geographically undesirable, but I asked if he might come to my suburb for dinner at a local, more casual, Spanish tapas restaurant. He agreed.

Jeff called about 15 minutes before he was supposed to arrive for our date, saying he had a flat tire on the tollway and would be a little late. What could I say? Sure, whenever you get here but, in my head, I was saying, "Great, he'll have to wait for AAA to come and change his tire, and he won't get here for another two hours. So much for the dinner plans." Lo and behold, about 35 minutes later, Jeff was at my door asking if he could wash his hands. I said, "What about your flat tire?" He replied, "I changed it." I responded incredulously and stupidly, "No!" Looking straight at me he said, "Check my trunk." Now, I was about to go on Date Two with a bald, middle-aged Jewish psychiatrist who could change a tire—if I hadn't just blown it. Jeff had instantly become a captivating combination of Sigmund Freud and Harrison Ford. We went out for a lovely dinner.

Date 2 was a hit for both of us. Our relationship quickly developed, and shortly thereafter, Jeff and I spent our first night together. Though I'm typically careful and obsessive in many areas of my life, I'm prone to throwing caution to the wind when it comes to intimate relationships.

After Jeff and I had dinner at a restaurant in my suburb, we went back to my house to watch a sporting event. Thankfully for both of us, sports were high on our priority list of things to watch on TV. However, Jeff wasn't shy about wanting to take the next step on the physical intimacy trail of our relationship. I don't know what I thought would happen when I invited Jeff back to my house that evening; at 37, I was still incredibly naïve. As we began to "make out," I quickly realized where this encounter was headed and said, "Whoa!" Jeff stopped, put his hands straight up in the air, and said if I wasn't comfortable, we would stop right there.

We took some time to talk about the next amorous step—how we'd be sharing our intimate pasts, including all the baggage that came with it. Not exactly romantic talk but adult talk. We slowly moved from the living room to the bedroom, taking our time, deliberate and gentle with each movement.

Jeff was tender and respectful and asked if he could stay the night. In the middle of the night, he didn't say, "Wow, that was great sex" or "You're so hot," instead, he whispered in my ear, *"Don't worry, I'll take care of you."* Who says that? At that moment, I wasn't trying to analyze the why of this declaration; I was just stunned and overcome by the closeness I felt for him. I had already come to understand this was not a man who pretended to be something he wasn't.

I did not, for one second, attach a more paternalistic interpretation to "Don't worry, I'll take care of you." I try not to be gender biased in any direction until I see a pattern of behavior convincing me otherwise. Jeff and I were in a moment in time, and I saw this statement as relational, reciprocal, something to build on. "Sometimes a cigar is just a cigar" as Sigmund Freud has been misquoted as saying. As I was completely caught off guard by this statement, but now smitten with Jeff, I ineloquently mumbled something about choking on the "L" word. Honest and transparent but, whoa, too much?

Jeff was quite sweet as he prepared to leave the following morning, but then I started down the ruminating path of "What did I just do?" After a night of romance would I regret not waiting and thinking this through, would I hear from him again, did he really care? After Jeff walked out the door, true dread began to set in, but it didn't last long. After about 10 seconds, my phone rang. It was Jeff calling from his car, asking, "So how was your date last night?" as if he were my best girlfriend. And there it was: *"Don't worry, I'll take care of you."* He understood my vulnerability and reached out to ease my mind. I laughed and relaxed. From that moment on, I knew in my heart I could trust Jeff, and he wouldn't hurt me. And he never did.

That was April 1992. We dated for several months, and then Jeff, his son Todd, and I started living together in November 1992. His older daughter, Jen, continued to live with Jeff's ex-wife. Jeff and I were married in June 1993 at the Spanish tapas restaurant where we had our second date.

***

Jeff and I had busy professional lives. He practiced child and adult psychiatry six days a week, sometimes seeing 50 patients in a week for 45-minute sessions. He was an expert witness in child custody cases, reviewed files for the State of Illinois involving the placement of children in special education environments, and provided clinical supervision for psychiatry residents at a large academic medical center. I was involved in teaching and academic administration at a nursing college that was more than 30 miles from the suburb where we lived.

Since I had no children of my own, I was also learning how to be a stepmom on the fly. Sometimes life unexpectedly takes something from you—like the chance to have children of your own—but gives you something in return. Early on in our life together as a family, I had no idea what I was doing as a parent, not a clue. Todd was almost 13 when we all started living with one another. I remember telling my friends at work that my fiancé had a soon-to-be 13-year-old son, and we'd all be living together soon. A couple of them said, "Oh, I'm sorry." Uh, what was that supposed to mean? They said, "Teenager, you'll see."

I'm lucky Todd was a good kid: smart, involved in school activities, and didn't go looking for trouble. But he was still a teenager, and I had no experience in being a parent. After a while, I decided looking at the mess in his room was not good for my mental health. We struggled over his desire and promptness to do chores. There was a great deal of grunting on his part and few words. This was all garden-variety teenage stuff, but I didn't know it. Not until Todd was 16 did I start to get the idea about teenagers—apparently, I'd forgotten I was one once, and I'm a slow learner the second time around.

One day when Todd was perhaps 14 or 15, I came home from work at the end of the day, and he was making his favorite pasta dinner. I felt bad I hadn't been home in time to make something for him, though my cooking could honestly be judged as poor to mediocre. I asked if we could sit down at the kitchen table and talk. I apologized we were such a busy family—all of us. Todd had joined the swim team and practice, which his dad drove him to in the morning, was at some ungodly hour. The kid got hungry earlier for dinner, no big surprise. Neither Jeff nor I could manage to be home on those days to fix him dinner or pick something up. Jeff would often work until 8 PM, so that was another dinner scheduling snafu.

In my apology, I said I was sorry we weren't more like Ozzy and Harriet, a 1950s and 1960s TV sitcom that had the stay-at-home mom and working dad. Harriet would prepare a wholesome dinner every night for her husband and their two sons. I kept talking and my son seemed to be listening intently, not saying much, as was his way. When I paused, he finally said, "I have a question for you?" Of course, the question was, "Who are Ozzy and Harriet?" Todd caught me off-guard; I wasn't expecting that response as I was so earnestly trying to connect with him. Aside from wanting to laugh so hard I could've fallen off my chair, I learned right then I wasn't even close to knowing how teenagers think.

Jeff was very patient with me as well as his son. We were all learning to navigate this new territory of a developing family. Jeff's children were an absolute priority for him, and he was certainly aware of the trauma of divorce. His kids would be no exception to that trauma just because their dad was a child psychiatrist. He did his best to be understanding and tolerant of us all.

Lisa Rosenberg

 The years passed by without us even knowing it. The kids went to college, got married, and had their own families. Jeff and I worked hard, saw friends, and went on vacation: nothing out of the ordinary. But our relationship as husband and wife deepened and evolved. The milestones of a maturing relationship—the graduations, weddings, births, illnesses, and deaths—all have a chapter in the book that was our marriage. But most of all, the constant thread was that we talked, we laughed, and we said, "I love you," a lot. I admired Jeff for his enormous integrity, and he said he learned some social graces from me. I was thankful for his presence in my life every day.

 Jeff passed away suddenly in May 2022, after we'd been together for 30 years. He left me stepchildren, whom I've come to regard as my own, and four grandchildren. I'm deeply grateful for these precious gifts, but I miss him terribly. Jeff taught me to try and be the best version of myself because he lived his life valuing what was important, namely, his family, friends, and patients.

 I guess one could draw different meanings from this story. For me, it was about taking a chance and co-creating a "big love" that immensely changed both of our lives. When you love someone deeply and authentically, the grief following their death is equally intense. But as I stand on the other side of the chasm that now divides us, I'm more convinced than ever that love is the essence of what truly matters.

Becoming Who We Are

Jeff was the American immigrant success story. Both of his parents emigrated from Eastern Europe in the early 1900s. They were part of a great wave of immigrants seeking a better life in America, where they might survive and, perhaps one day, thrive. Jeff's mother, Leibe Silberstein, Leibe anglicized to Lillian, was born in Kalish, Poland in 1910. She left Poland for America in 1921 on a ship named Estonia. Severe economic hardship and food shortages were prevalent across Eastern Europe, as was rampant anti-Semitism. Lillian was only 11 years old when she journeyed alone for her voyage to America, traveling in steerage, the lowest possible category of long-distance steamship passage. The steerage area of the ship was a large space located below decks near the steering gear, where living conditions were overcrowded and unsanitary, and the food barely edible.

Lillian lived with an older brother and sister in Poland, as both their parents and grandparents had died. The children were shuttled from one relative to another, whoever could care for them for a period of time. In later life, Lillian recalled a terrifying incident when she was quite young and her father was still alive. The family was hurriedly traveling in a wagon, her father fleeing from an attack by people who were shooting arrows at them. Lillian may very well have been recalling a pogrom, a violent ethnic attack particularly aimed at Jewish people which, unfortunately, was not uncommon in Eastern Europe in the late 19th and early 20th centuries. In 1919, two years before Lillian came to America, nearly 100,000 Jews were murdered in Ukraine and Poland in pogroms. Headlines across the globe reported these ethnic killings, with aid workers warning that millions of Jews were in danger of complete extermination. These grim predictions came true two decades later.

Conditions were dire, but there was money to send only one of the three Silberstein children to America. The family decided it would be Lillian since she was the youngest, even though the minimum age for unaccompanied travel was 12. Her two older siblings, only teenagers themselves, felt they had a better chance to survive the hardships of their homeland. Lillian's siblings never made it to America after Lillian arrived. When she was 16, Lillian's family in America got a letter from Poland telling them her sister had died. Over the years that followed, Lillian got an occasional postcard from her brother. Just before World War II began, Lillian's husband worked fervently to find and bring her brother to America, but to no avail. He was never heard from again, likely murdered during the Holocaust.

Lillian was sponsored to come to America by an aunt and uncle who were living in New York City. They were already supporting a family with six children. Lillian's Aunt Sarah and Uncle Jacob had to obtain a $75 bond for Lillian to guarantee she had someone responsible for her in the U.S. In addition, they had to sign an affidavit swearing they could support Lillian and that their yearly income was at least $2000. It was unlikely this was true. Jacob, Sarah, and their children lived in a tiny Bronx apartment and were dirt poor. Lillian would end up sleeping on a cot in the kitchen.

It's hard to imagine an 11-year-old child traveling alone to the U.S., not speaking a word of English. Traveling conditions in steerage were harsh—cramped and crowded quarters and little fresh air, with travelers often bringing their own bedding and food. The trip likely took 10 to 14 days. Upon arrival at the Port of New York, Ellis Island immigrants entered a large room in the main building, the Registry Room, with a series of long, wooden benches. It was here that an immigrant's name would be called, and they would be questioned: Where were you born? How much money do you have? Can you support yourself? Do you know anyone in this country? Depending on their answers, an immigrant would either be admitted to the U.S. or denied entry. If they made it through this first phase, immigrants still needed to pass a physical and mental examination. If it was determined the individual had a permanent disability or incurable disease that would keep them from earning a living, they were sent back home. An immigrant's fate largely depended on whether they or someone else could provide financial support.

Jeff's father, Abraham (Abe), arrived in America several months after Lillian. His journey was somewhat different, but every bit as harrowing. Abe was born in Nemyriv, a town that is now in Ukraine, but in the early 1900s, it was still part of Russia. When the Russian Revolution occurred in 1917, Ukraine declared its independence. However, after World War I, Ukraine was partitioned between Bolshevik Russia and Poland. In 1921, post-czarist Russia was still mired in severe economic hardship and long-standing anti-Semitism.

Abe's father, Morris Zapopnik, had left for America eight years earlier in 1913. He was to earn enough money as a tailor to sponsor his wife, Hannah, and two young sons—11-year-old Abe and 9-year-old Aaron—to join him in his newly adopted country. The average weekly income for an immigrant tailor might have been $8 to $10. A ticket to travel in steerage from Eastern Europe to New York City was $30 to $35, equivalent in today's dollars to $450 to $550. Morris sent for his family once he had saved enough money to buy three steamship passage tickets and satisfied the other financial requirements.

The journey to reach the port city from which Abe and his family would depart took three months of arduous travel. Hannah and her two boys traveled on foot through the countryside with whatever belongings they could carry. With little money, the family slept out in the open, sometimes taking shelter in a ditch if they feared for their safety. Food was scarce and a hasty meal might've been stealthily acquired from a nearby garden.

    Upon arriving to board the steamer to take them to America, it coincidentally turned out to be the Estonia, the same ship that transported Lillian to her new home. Hannah, Abe, and Aaron also went through immigration at Ellis Island, NY, met the requisite standards to enter the U.S., and were allowed to step foot on American soil. When the family was reunited, Hannah, Abe, and Aaron discovered their last name was no longer Zapopnik. When Morris went through Ellis Island, it was not uncommon for new last names to be given to immigrants so they sounded more "American." Thus, Zapopnik became Spector. An interesting side note is that Abe's brother, Aaron, came to dislike his given birth name and changed it to Harry, feeling it sounded more American.

    As the saying goes, timing is everything in life. Anti-immigrant sentiment had been growing in the U.S. since around 1875. In the late 1800s, several laws were enacted to restrict persons of Chinese descent from entering the U.S. The focus shifted to southern and eastern European immigrants in 1921 and 1924. Particularly, the Immigration Act of 1924 limited total annual immigration and enacted quotas based on immigrant nationality favoring northern and western European countries, as people from those areas were considered more "desirable." According to the Department of State at the time, the act's purpose was "to preserve the ideal of U.S. homogeneity." This story may never have been written had Jeff's parents tried to enter the U.S. after 1921. By 1943, a little over 20 years later, almost every Jewish person in Nemyriv had been murdered by the Nazis.

    Life was anything but easy for immigrants coming to this country in the 1920s. Anti-immigrant sentiment was only growing. Poverty and crowded living conditions were the norm, and working long, hard hours was essential to survive. Jeff's father might have attended school for a year when he arrived in New York City but, by age 12, he was already working to help support the family. Jeff's mother needed to help in the home of her aunt and uncle—cleaning, cooking, and washing clothes so that others in the household could work. Neither of Jeff's parents finished high school in the U.S. Though there were truancy laws regarding school attendance, they applied only to children between the ages of eight and twelve. Children 12 to 14 could receive a work permit if their parents gave permission. However, the enforcement of these laws was often quite lenient. When Jeff's father had finally established his own business after many years of arduous labor, he was adamant his children should "have a childhood," as his had been sacrificed.

In 1930, Abe met Lillian. Abe was immediately attracted to Lillian, but she didn't appear interested. Lillian was in love with another young man. However, a serious problem arose for Abe's rival. The young man Lillian was in love with contracted tuberculosis, frequently referred to at the time as "consumption." Modern treatments for TB weren't available in the 1920s, and TB was often deadly. If someone contracted TB and did survive, it was likely their disease would remain communicable. Treatment commonly involved confinement in a TB sanatorium, where patients focused on rest, exercise, and maintaining a healthy diet. Lillian's family warned her against a future with this man. In those days, parents held great sway over their children's major life decisions, particularly regarding marriage. Lillian acquiesced and stopped the relationship. She then turned her attention to Abe who was patiently waiting.

Before their marriage in 1931, Abe gave Lillian a priceless gift. In April 1930, Jeff's mother completed a Declaration of Intention form—also known as "first papers"—the initial step in the process of becoming a United States citizen at that time. However, the form required Lillian to record her birth date. Lillian didn't know the actual day she was born, so Abe gave her a birthdate, Nov. 10, 1910. In recounting this story, Jeff thought it was one of the most romantic things he'd ever heard. This may be an apocryphal story, but it had a profound effect nonetheless. For all his sharp wit and intelligence, Jeff was a romantic at heart. He loved that his father gave his mother the gift of her birthdate—a unique and precious gift that can only be given once.

In April 1931, Abe and Lillian were married. It's important to recall that the Great Depression began in 1929 and lasted approximately 10 years. The unemployment rate exceeded 20% at times, and bread lines were common. But somehow, people still lived their lives, fell in love, got married, and raised families. Considering the challenges they faced, it's remarkable to reflect on the strength of will Abe and Lillian needed to move forward, despite being given no advantage.

After they married, the young couple continued to live and work in New York City. Abe worked with his brother, Harry, as a sign painter. Lillian, good with numbers, took some courses and learned to become a bookkeeper. Together, they made enough money to start a family. In October 1932, Abe and Lillian had their first child, Beverly. Four years later, in 1936, they had another daughter, Rita.

According to a family story, Jeff's mother was mugged in 1940 as she made her way to get her husband's watch repaired. Two men accosted her, hit her on the head with a wrench, and knocked her unconscious. The two men who assaulted her laid her body out by the trolley tracks, stealing the watch and her jewelry. The police came to Abe's door (they didn't have a telephone) and told him his wife had been mugged and was at a local hospital.

Abe, by all accounts, was known to be a quiet man. He didn't get angry or raise his voice much and wasn't prone to emotional outbursts. But, as the story goes, Abe would not let this rest. The police were unlikely to pursue this case with any vigor, so he searched

Adventure on Joyland Road

the local pool halls for information or evidence about who perpetrated this crime against his wife. In his search, he entered a pool hall one day and found a man wearing his watch. Abe proceeded to beat the man up and take his watch back. Abe was no more than 5'6" inches tall, but that didn't stop him from seeking his own justice.

Whether all or part of this story is true, it has been passed down as a piece of family history. And that's what children learn—values, behaviors, and principles of how you live your life. I always wondered why Jeff was so protective of me, in ways that often surprised me. Here we were, modern Americans in the 20th and 21st centuries, educated professionals, with him being a psychiatrist, no less. And yet, every time Jeff sensed another man "sniffing" around me, he made certain they knew he was there. I believe Jeff learned this behavior from his father. Family stories, whether factual or embellished, are true in those families and are powerful vectors in shaping behavior.

As the Spector family was establishing itself in its new homeland, Eastern Europe was thrust into the darkness and horrors of World War II. In 1940, all men in the U.S., ages 18 to 64, had to register for the draft; however, married men were exempt. Though Abe didn't have to serve as a soldier in the military, he was called to work as an electrician in the U.S. Navy Brooklyn shipyard, which he did until 1945 when the war ended. Jeff was born in November 1944.

In 1946, Abe decided it was time to move his family out of New York City. He wanted to start his own sign-making business and decided Monticello, New York was the place for him and his wife to raise their young family. In those early days in Monticello, business was tough to come by, but Abe persisted. He saw a steady increase in customers when other sign-making businesses in town closed. Abe specialized in making neon signs which were popular in that era.

Though Monticello is only 90 minutes north of New York City, it was still a rural setting in 1946. Abe went to Monticello without his wife and bought a home for his family on Cottage Street. Unfortunately, Lillian wasn't particularly fond of it. She understood why Abe bought it; they could rent some rooms to supplement their income. Not long after, Abe purchased a different home on Hammond Street, much to his wife's chagrin. It had a choppy layout, and Jeff's room was the size of a large closet that could only fit a single bed and was attached to his parent's bedroom.

Jeff, a healthy, blonde, blue-eyed child, was meant to be a city boy. Though his small, pastoral town of 5,000 was only 90 minutes from New York City, it felt like a world away. His town was part of the Borscht Belt resort area in upstate New York, popular with Jewish city dwellers from the 1920s through the 1960s. Monticello's population, along with those of the neighboring towns, grew exponentially in the summer months, exploding with visitors from the city escaping the heat—at a time when neither air conditioning nor air travel was as common as it became in the latter half of the 1900s.

Abe and Lillian were adamant about Jeff getting an education. Almost every Jewish parent from that era wanted their child to be educated in a profession, with physicians, lawyers, and accountants being the most popular parental choices. While in high school, Jeff told his father he might want to become a math teacher, since he was gifted mathematically. Abe responded, "If you want to become a math teacher, do it after you go to medical school."

During the summer months, Abe's business picked up as the local merchants were busy trying to attract the swell of tourists. Jeff helped his father during the summer, carrying ladders and doing some of the heavier work. Though Jeff was interested in all things mechanical, Abe wasn't anxious to teach his son the business of sign-making. Jeff would say, "Dad, if you teach me, I can help you more." Abe didn't want his son to entertain any ideas about his future other than becoming a medical doctor. The less he taught him the skill of neon sign-making, the better.

Adventure on Joyland Road

Jeff's mother also had ideas about her son's future and how she might protect him from forces beyond his control. However, the traumatic pasts of both her and her husband skewed those ideas. Jeff played a musical instrument as a child and through adolescence. He was compelled to do so by his mother. He might not have minded as much if it had been an instrument more to his liking, but it was an accordion—big, bulky, and uncool. When he felt old enough to protest, it was to no avail. His mother's logic went like this: if her son played an instrument, he could join the czar's marching band instead of being forced to fight on the front lines. Knowing the roots of his mother's deep fear, Jeff never had the heart to tell her there were no accordion players in the czar's or anyone else's marching band.

Probably, with great anxiety experienced by his mother, Jeff was drafted into the Navy under the Berry plan during the Vietnam era. Under this plan, because Jeff was training to be a physician, his induction into the military would be delayed until he had completed his first year of a general internship in medicine and his psychiatry residency. Though promised by the Navy he could finish his three-year residency in adult psychiatry, after the first year, Jeff was called up. He was relatively newly married, so he, his wife, and their fastidious St. Bernard, Murray, would be uprooted from Boston and have to adapt to a new environment and military life. From every angle, this was an unplanned disruption in Jeff's life.

Before leaving for his assignment, the military liaison officer told Jeff, "Doc, you're going to love where you've been assigned, it's halfway between L.A. and San Francisco." This individual failed to mention that the exact location was the Lemoore Naval Air Station in the San Joaquin Valley, where the summertime temperature could reach 110 degrees. The closest city was Fresno, CA. Jeff entered the Navy in 1973 with the rank of Lieutenant and was honorably discharged in 1975 as a Lieutenant Commander. He spent the entirety of his time stationed at Lemoore doing psychiatric evaluations, never once stepping onto a naval vessel. After his discharge, Jeff completed his residency in adult psychiatry in Boston, and then pursued a fellowship in child and adolescent psychiatry in Chicago.

Jeff had ambivalence about his time in the military, and at first, never talked much about it. The Vietnam War was unpopular at home, particularly among young people; protests against the war in Vietnam were common. When soldiers returned home, traumatized by their experience in Vietnam, they were often met with disdain for having served in an unpopular war. Feeling unwelcome upon their return only made the adjustment to civilian life more difficult.

After many years, a brief encounter changed how Jeff felt about his time in the military. We were on a flight home from California after a visit to Big Sur, the Redwoods, and all that is beautiful along Highway 1 of the West Coast. Our aisle had three seats across—Jeff sat in the aisle seat, I was in the middle, and a sailor in uniform occupied the window seat. This was still the age when people talked to each other on an airplane and didn't have their noses buried in electronic devices. I struck up a conversation with this young, fresh-faced sailor sitting next to me who hailed from a small town in mid-America. There wasn't a hint of cynicism or unkindness about him; just an earnest, sweet boy who was alone and far from home.

I asked where he was stationed in the Navy. He said New London, Connecticut. To this point in the conversation, Jeff hadn't looked in our direction nor said one word. Jeff turned to the young sailor and stated matter-of-factly, "Sub School." The young man's eyes widened in amazement as he asked, "How did you know that?" The U.S. Navy's submarine training school for enlisted sailors, Basic Enlisted Submarine School (BESS), is located in Groton, New London County, Connecticut.

Having always been proud of my husband's service to his country, I quickly interjected that Jeff was a Navy veteran. The sailor, wanting to know more, asked at what rank Jeff had been discharged from the Navy. Jeff explained he was drafted as a commissioned officer during the Vietnam era and was honorably discharged as a Lieutenant Commander. The young sailor's eyes widened even more, if it were physically possible. He sat up straight in his seat and saluted my husband. He then extended his hand to Jeff and said, "Thank you for your service, sir."

It was hard to catch Jeff off-guard, but this kid did. He was genuinely surprised to hear such respect and appreciation for his military service; it was before regular public displays of gratitude for active military and veterans became more commonplace. When that started happening at concerts and sporting events in the late 1990s and early 2000s—asking veterans to stand and be acknowledged—I would have to nudge Jeff to his feet, as he didn't think he deserved it.

When Jeff was first drafted, he considered his options: leave the U.S., apply as a conscientious objector (CO), or serve. One particular experience helped him make up his mind. He spoke with a CO organization, and they asked him whether he would physically take up arms to defend his family if they came under threat. Without hesitating, Jeff replied yes. Because of his answer to that question, the CO organizer said he didn't believe Jeff would be a good fit to claim conscientious objector status to the war.

Jeff's answer to that query settled his internal debate about his decision—he would serve. Jeff would never assume a false moral ground no matter the personal cost. Over time, he gained some perspective on his military service and began to feel proud that he had served his country when called. In 1973, Jeff may not have liked having his life disrupted by a divisive war, but his integrity was something he was never willing to compromise.

***

Jeff believed he was meant to leave rural, small-town life and felt it at a young age. When his parents took him to New York City as a young boy, they warned him about how loud it would be—traffic all night, horns honking, people on the streets at all hours. When Jeff went to his room on that momentous first night, as soon as he entered, he went straight to the window and opened it to hear the cacophony of city noise he longed for.

In the 1950s, parents were less fearful their children would encounter trouble if they sent them off without adult supervision, even to New York City. It was a two-hour excursion from Monticello to the city. Jeff got braces to straighten his teeth when he was about 11 or 12. His orthodontist's office was near Grand Central Station in midtown Manhattan. After accompanying Jeff to the doctor's office a few times, his mother believed her smart, young son would do just fine taking the bus from Monticello to the Port Authority in New York City, then boarding a train to Grand Central Station. From there, he could make the short walk to the orthodontist's office. Jeff, eager to travel solo into the city, gladly agreed it was an excellent idea and that he could handle it. However, things didn't go exactly as planned.

After Jeff got off the bus at the Port Authority Bus Terminal, instead of taking the train to Midtown Manhattan, he mistakenly took a train uptown to Harlem. When he stepped off the train, he realized his mistake. Here was this kid from a small town in upstate New York, so eager to be on his own in the big city, yet now, completely unprepared as to what to do next. He began to panic but then, being the smart kid he was, he figured out what he could do. He approached two older African American women and said tentatively, "This isn't Grand Central Station, is it?" to which they replied, "No, honey, it isn't. You just stay with us, and we'll get you on the right train." And that is exactly what they did. Jeff got to his appointment in Midtown, boarded the correct train home, and didn't breathe a word of his misadventure to his mother, knowing she would never let him hazard off by himself into the city again.

Adventure on Joyland Road

Jeff eventually left Monticello to attend Union College, a small liberal arts institution in Schenectady, New York (about 120 miles from Monticello). While at college, at the age of 20 and in his sophomore year, Jeff got a call from his mother. His parents had been visiting his married sisters who both lived in Florida. Lillian and Abe stayed with their youngest daughter, Rita, for a short time, but Abe wanted to make sure his wife had a real Florida vacation. After visiting Rita, they headed for Miami Beach. But the next day, at the age of 54, Abe suffered a massive heart attack in the bathroom of a Miami Beach hotel. He died almost instantly. The day before, Rita remembers seeing her parents sitting on the grass in her backyard, holding hands, heads together, as if they were sharing secrets like two high school sweethearts. Jeff left school immediately and returned to Monticello for his father's funeral.

Jeff, just like his dad had hoped, went on to attend Albert Einstein Medical School in the Bronx. He accepted a first-year internship at Mary Imogine Bassett Hospital in Cooperstown, New York, home of the National Baseball Museum. During this time, Jeff's mother became ill; she was diagnosed with colon cancer. In the late 1960s and early 1970s, screening exams, like colonoscopies, weren't nearly as common, nor were the greater variety of treatment options available today. Thus, colon cancer had much poorer mortality outcomes. Despite seeking treatment at Memorial Sloan-Kettering Cancer Center in New York City, Lillian succumbed to her disease in 1970, passing away at age 60. She's buried next to her loving husband in Monticello.

It seems Jeff's parents did so much living on this earth in so short a time. Their lives were defined by hardship, battling every step of the way to establish themselves and their family in a new world, trying to taste a little of the sweet life.

Jeff never left New York State until he started his psychiatry residency in Boston at Beth Israel Hospital. Sometimes, small-town life keeps a hold on people until they're ready to spread their wings. Though Jeff always liked the idea of being in a big city and experiencing everything it had to offer, ironically, our vacation getaways were usually to places where nature abounded. He seemed to prefer towering trees over soaring skyscrapers and the sound of ocean waves lapping the shore to the hum of city life. Jeff never lost his love for the rolling hills of his childhood upstate New York. Before he took me to Monticello and the surrounding area for his 50th high school reunion, he said, "You don't know how beautiful it is." He was right. It was early autumn and dense forests were beginning to turn into a cascade of color. It was stunningly picturesque.

    The history of my husband's family is not uncommon. So many people came to this country as poor immigrants, facing extraordinary odds and experiencing profound trauma. One mishap, one misfortune, one missed connection changes the entire trajectory of a family. That's what makes each story in the frame of history so unique and astonishing. These accounts are the life stories people tell and their families continue to tell—the stories that shape how we become who we are. It is the personal lore we hand down to the next generation, hoping they cherish it as we did. When our stories are remembered, taken out, and dusted off from the distant corners where they rest, we and all the brave, determined people who came before us are not forgotten.

When Everything Changed in an Instant

I woke up Friday morning May 20, 2022, around 6:00 am, having slept soundly during the night. On Thursday, Jeff and I had a long day driving to and from downtown Chicago for an appointment, and we both were beat. I'm not much of a sound sleeper these days, but I was on the night of May 19. I said Jeff's name softly, so as not to startle him. Our cleaning ladies were coming in about an hour, and I wanted to give him enough time to get out of bed and get dressed. I looked at Jeff and said his name a few more times, but he didn't move. Then I called his name loudly, but he didn't respond. I nudged his shoulder and started screaming his name. Nothing, no response. And then, I knew the thing I dreaded most—the stuff of my worst nightmares—had happened. When you're aging in place with someone, you allow yourself brief moments of what the end might look like: prolonged illness, sudden cardiac arrest, or a tragic accident. When these fleeting thoughts came to mind, I was thinking in terms of probable outcomes. Many older adults become ill, and loved ones have some warning, some ability to prepare for a distant or not-so-distant death. That is not what happened here.

I jumped to my phone and called 911 before I got to the other side of the bed. I was so panicked, I hung up on the 911 operator after providing my address. I touched Jeff's skin—it was cool. I didn't bother to check his pulse or breathing; I could already tell there would be no beat to feel, no breath to detect. We have an automated external defibrillator (AED) in our building, so I threw on my robe, ran to get it, and rushed back to my apartment. Now 911 was calling back and, at the same time, I was trying to figure out how to get the AED working. I have never experienced more heart-pounding, brain-paralyzing terror than in that moment. After getting the AED paddles in place, I pushed the button to administer the shock, but nothing happened. I tried again—no shock. I had never used an AED before and didn't remember that it won't deliver a shock if it can't detect a shockable rhythm, like ventricular fibrillation. I thought I was doing something wrong.

    I then started administering CPR, screaming to the 911 dispatcher the paramedics needed to hurry—my husband was dead. The dispatcher told me to get my husband on the floor, then start CPR. Get him on the floor? Jeff weighed just under 200 pounds. I weigh in at 110. I couldn't waste time figuring out how to get him safely on the floor. Didn't she understand—he's dead—I have to start CPR now! I knew to deliver chest compressions with force and quickly, but I could feel myself tiring. For God's sake, where were the paramedics? I continued to do CPR until the paramedics arrived. I tried to save Jeff's life, and so did the paramedics, but it was too late. He had died sometime in the night. They called the code after 20 minutes.

    While the paramedics were working on Jeff, the police arrived. When someone dies at home, the police, with the help of the paramedics and a phone call to the coroner, determine if the cause of death was due to natural circumstances. So, there you stand, in a state of complete shock and disbelief, having to provide a coherent medical history and explain what medications your spouse was taking. I removed a small plastic box containing Jeff's medications from a cabinet shelf. I slid the box toward the police officer so she could sift through it.

    In the midst of all this, I called my good friend and neighbor in the building, Iris, who is also a nurse. I told her what had just happened and asked if she could come to me. Though early in the morning, she wasn't home; I'd reached her while she was in her car. Wherever she was headed so early, she turned around and came to my apartment with her husband. When she walked through the door, she gave me what I needed most at that moment—open arms to fall into and fall apart in.

When the police determined no criminal intent had occurred to cause my husband's demise, they said I needed to call a funeral home—now. I was dumbfounded. I was in a state of shock with little to no ability to think, but they insisted the call needed to happen immediately. I only knew of two Jewish funeral homes in my area. With Iris standing by my side, I sat down at my computer and opened the funeral home websites. The first said they did burials and cremations, the other only listed burials. Sitting there in my robe, weary and beyond any ability to take in what had just happened, I arranged for the first local funeral home to pick up Jeff—but only after his son had a chance to come to the house to say goodbye. Plunged into chaotic and overwhelming grief, this was the first of many decisions I needed to make in the next 24 hours.

The paramedics and police quietly left after I finished the brief call to the funeral home, mumbling condolences on their way out. Over the next month, I would find remnants of the paramedics' visit in my bedroom: an abandoned plastic syringe cap that had rolled aimlessly under the bed, a stray alcohol wipe wrapper, dried drips of various administered fluids that failed to save my husband's life. All were grim reminders of what had happened that morning and how everything had changed in an instant.

I then had to make the first of many difficult phone calls to let Jeff's family know he had suddenly passed away. Of course, Jeff's children were the first calls. How do you tell your children that their father, who seemed fine yesterday, is now gone? No warning, no last goodbyes, just gone. There's no way to sugarcoat this awful event.

"Todd, I have terrible news, your dad passed away last night." I heard Todd catch his breath, but no words came. I told him what had happened in the last 30 minutes and that he needed to come right away. I wouldn't let the funeral home take Jeff until Todd had a chance to say goodbye.

After I reached Todd and he was on his way, I immediately called Jeff's daughter, who lives in California. I must've called a few dozen times over the next 90 minutes. Because of the two-hour time difference, it was early morning on the West Coast, and her phone was on "Do Not Disturb." She finally picked up, not knowing I'd called so many times. Again, I had to repeat the shocking and horrific statement, "Jen, I have terrible news, your dad passed away last night." Jen began to cry and couldn't believe the words I just said.

It took Todd quite a while to get to our home in the suburbs from where he lives in the city. Traffic is never good, and so it was on this day, too. When he arrived, Todd came into the bedroom to be with his father for a few moments. I then stayed close to Jeff as he lay motionless on the floor, touching his face and beard. When it was time, I kissed Jeff goodbye. Letting him go was unbearable. Todd and I accompanied the gurney out of the building and into the awaiting funeral home vehicle.

It was important to me that Jeff's funeral service be officiated by a rabbi, even though we weren't particularly religious nor did we belong to a synagogue. One of the first phone calls I made that morning was to Rabbi Dave, who lives in my building. Jeff and I had come to know Rabbi Dave over the years. He and Jeff had quite a bit in common; they both hailed from New York and served in the military. Rabbi Dave and I often had long conversations by our community pool in the summer, talking about books, politics—you name it. I told Rabbi Dave what had occurred earlier in the morning. Before I could get the request out of my mouth, Rabbi Dave said he would be honored to officiate at the chapel service. Without my having to say it, he understood the enormous pain I was in and my need for support; whether I was religious or not didn't matter. This was the first of many kindnesses Rabbi Dave would bestow upon me. He was, and continues to be, an amazing friend.

At 2 PM that afternoon, Todd and I sat in the funeral home waiting to meet with one of the funeral directors. We would put Jen on speakerphone when the meeting started. Led by the funeral director, Todd and I descended some steps to a lower-level conference room. As we walked a narrow hallway to the room, I could see a little further down the corridor to a larger, darkened room where the caskets were displayed. I shuddered at the thought of Jeff being placed in one but kept that thought to myself.

This felt beyond unreal; outwardly, I was moving and speaking, but inside, I was drowning in an ocean of anguish. How could this be happening? How could Jeff be dead, just like that? I was about to be asked a bunch of questions about my husband's funeral service and the disposition of his body—he was alive 24 hours ago. No. No way. This cannot be happening.

You might wonder if Jeff was ill or declining in some way, did I have an inkling of what was about to occur? Jeff underwent major cardiac surgery in May 2019, followed by a complicated recovery. Within a couple of months after the surgery, he decided to retire from practicing psychiatry after a career of almost 50 years. I retired in September 2019 from my role as associate dean at a nursing college. Jeff completed his cardiac rehab program in December 2019 and was doing pretty well. Then, the COVID pandemic hit in April 2020, so we laid low like everyone else.

We were finding our way through being newly retired. We had both worked non-stop throughout our adult lives, so this new, free-range lifestyle was a huge adjustment—perhaps more so for me than Jeff. However, COVID gave us a lot of time together, something that likely wouldn't have happened otherwise. In the six months prior to his death, Jeff seemed more fatigued and less exercise-tolerant. But when we visited his cardiologist the month before he died, all of his lab tests and echocardiogram were within normal limits. The weekend before he died, we drove up and back to Omaha for a wedding. He went to the dentist the day before to have a crown replaced. It felt like we were living a normal life.

As many couples do as they get older, Jeff and I talked about whether he wanted to be buried or cremated. When no terminal event is imminently on the horizon, these conversations are "arms-length," with emotions detached—a what-if, down-the-line discussion. It turned out to be an important and prescient conversation. His response to the question of whether he would prefer to be cremated or buried is one of the most selfless I've ever heard. He said the decision regarding the disposition of his remains should be made by the living, based on what would bring them the most comfort. I told him I was leaning towards cremation, as I didn't know if I could let him go so quickly after his death. Cremation would give me the option of keeping his ashes. He said that was fine, just make sure he was really dead first.

Cremation was my decision (after consulting with Rabbi Dave), along with military honors at his funeral. I also had to choose the flowers for the service and the lacquered box for his ashes. I edited the obituary written by the funeral director and grappled with the many details involved in honoring the person you loved most in this world. All of these decisions were made within eight hours of Jeff's death. Though Todd, Jen, and I discussed each choice, they deferred to my wishes. I was grateful for that. The surreal task of making these choices, when the worst thing in the world had just happened to us, remains inconceivable.

The next day I began calling close friends and family who I thought would want to attend the chapel service in person or livestream it. I didn't leave this task to the kids or send emails. I called everyone. Why would I have undertaken such a seemingly difficult task? At the time, I didn't think about why I chose to be the messenger to inform people of Jeff's death, but I believe I understand my motivation now. Because Jeff died so suddenly, I think I needed to say those words—"I have terrible news, Jeff passed away"—over and over to other people so the reality of his death might begin to sink in. I needed their shock and disbelief to normalize my feelings and hear their heartfelt condolences and recollections to soothe me.

    Three days later, before the funeral service began, I sat with my grandchildren in the chapel. We looked at photos on my phone of their grandfather and talked about how much he loved them. One of my grandchildren said then, and still does, "Grandpa was the best hugger." As friends and family entered the funeral home, I stood at the front of the chapel, greeting and talking to those who came, keen for their comfort and compassion. Once the line of greeters had diminished, I looked around the chapel. Mourners sat in various parts of the large chapel, perhaps making an internal calculation that their chosen seat was a reflection of their closeness to Jeff and me. Others, less comfortable with death and loss, may have opted to distance themselves—both physically and emotionally—from the front of the chapel.

    I noticed one man wearing a mask, who was sitting by himself far off to one side. He hadn't come to the front of the chapel earlier to offer his condolences. I knew who he was, and I went over to him. It was a former patient of Jeff's. This was someone who had a special relationship with my husband. This man had been a patient of Jeff's as a child and continued therapy with him as he grew older and started his own family. Jeff and I attended his wedding. Even after Jeff retired, a few former patients would occasionally call him to talk or invite him to lunch; this man was one of them. I knew he'd be extremely upset by Jeff's sudden death, and he was. His eyes were red from crying, and he could barely speak. I thanked him for coming and reminded him of the deep and caring connection he and Jeff had. At that moment, I believed this man needed me as much as I needed him.

Once I sat down, the service started with military honors. As composed as I thought I was greeting everyone as they flowed into the chapel, I became undone as soon as the service got underway. Three members of a Navy honor detail were present to perform a ceremony, which included a bugler playing Taps and the folding and presentation of the American flag to me. At the beginning of the playing of Taps, everyone needed to stand. I could barely raise myself from the seat without the help of my son. When we sat down, I watched the honor guards fold the flag in front of where I was seated. One of the young officers knelt directly facing me, handed me the flag, and said he was sorry for my loss. Trembling, I took the flag from him and laid it on my lap. I was beyond any state of being I had ever imagined. I was being crushed by the solemn reality of my husband's death.

Rabbi Dave began with an introduction and a few words. His prayers and reflections about Jeff would come later in the service; first would be the eulogies from his family. The children and I chose to eulogize Jeff at his funeral, each of us taking a turn to speak. I'd thought this through the day before. I imagined it would be hard—really hard—but I thought I could rely on my usual fortitude to read a page and a half about my late husband in front of my family and friends. What I couldn't envision was my current state of utter devastation. Now, I didn't know if I could even stand upright.

With every fiber of my being, I was determined to express who Jeff was, his dedication to family, friends, and patients, his amazing sense of humor, and his love of telling stories. I told the mourners Jeff's parents were immigrants to this country who came with nothing, worked hard, and built a life so their son could attend college and medical school. In one generation, the entire trajectory of a family was altered; it's the American success story, and one worth telling. Hard as it was, I told his story and am glad I did. The children and I wanted Jeff to be honored and remembered by others in a way that only intimate recollections from loved ones could provide. I would've sacrificed anything to do it—and in retrospect, I would do it again.

After the chapel service, we returned home to begin the first structured period of mourning, shiva. The main purpose of the tradition of "sitting shiva," is to create an environment of comfort and community for mourners. The period of sitting shiva is traditionally a week in length. Many less traditional followers of Judaism sit for two to three days. Whatever timeframe is chosen, mourners gather in the family's home to offer their condolences and support.

People came from the chapel to my building where we were sitting shiva. But others dropped by, too. Friends, colleagues, and patients of Jeff's, my friends and colleagues (some of whom I hadn't seen in a few years), and neighbors from the building came to pay their respects. Friends and family took care of all the arrangements for food and beverages for the two-day shiva. Everyone wanted me to eat, thinking I was neglecting myself. I just wanted to talk with everyone who came, amazed and grateful for their kindness. After the last day of shiva, my daughter stayed with me for a few more days to help, and more importantly, so I wasn't alone. Eventually, I had to face being alone, but in those first few days, it was a godsend to have her there.

Over the next several months, I wrestled with what to do with Jeff's ashes. I didn't know Jeff would die so suddenly, but I was right about my need to keep his ashes with me for a while. I just couldn't see myself burying him and walking away from the gravesite; that disuniting from him was more than I could endure. I needed him with me in our house—to talk to and cry with—so I might find some way to keep putting one foot in front of the other. Later, I write about how the irrational lives right next door to the rational in your head. In this very personal journey, you do what you need to do to find your way through.

During this time, I contemplated having Jeff buried in a national military cemetery that is about a mile and a half away from where I live. Counter to that, I also thought about keeping his ashes forever. But forever is the forever of my lifetime. What would happen after that? I didn't make a final decision but continued to gather information from the cemetery about their burial process. The cemetery grounds were undergoing some changes—certain burial sections offering more privacy and space would soon be filled— and it weighed heavily on me about what I should do and when to do it.

After six months, I decided to bury Jeff's ashes in the national cemetery. I'd begun to feel the longer I held onto his ashes, the harder it was going to be to give them up. I could easily visit him, and my ashes would be buried alongside his. It was also important for me to make a decision in perpetuity for both of us.

The last, and perhaps most important, reason for burying Jeff in a national cemetery didn't occur to me right away. It took about a year to verbalize this last, driving motivation—I didn't want Jeff ever to be forgotten. In a national cemetery, he never will be. He will be honored on Memorial Day and Veteran's Day, and a wreath is laid at each veteran's headstone in December. The grounds are meticulously cared for with lush, weedless grass surrounding the headstones. Visitors who know no one specifically buried there, come to this historic place to pay their respects. There's some comfort in knowing that.

I wasn't ready when the day came for the arranged burial of Jeff's ashes. It was a raw, windy afternoon, cold and sleeting. Once again, displaying his compassion, Rabbi Dave accompanied me on this harsh day to say the mourner's Kaddish, the Jewish prayer traditionally recited in memory of the dead. I made certain I had dinner that evening with good friends in my condo building, so I wasn't alone.

It took several months for Jeff's headstone to be placed. The cemetery administrator, Kelly, whom I'd come to know over the months of deciding to bury Jeff in a national cemetery, told me I needed to provide the headstone inscription within 10 days after the burial. In six to eight weeks, the headstone would be completed and placed. Three months went by, but still no headstone appeared. I called Kelly and asked what was happening. She said a headstone did arrive but the stone was chipped, so she sent it back to be re-done. A second chipped headstone arrived, and Kelly sent that one back, too. She said she wouldn't accept the headstone until it was perfect. And when the third one arrived it was, indeed, perfect. Kelly was a wonderful advocate, showing great respect for the person being buried and keeping me, as his spouse, from being further wounded.

The inscription I created for Jeff's headstone reads: "Beloved husband, father, friend, and physician." Besides the standard information on a veteran's headstone (name, dates of birth and death, military rank, and service during a war), I was allowed three lines, 15 characters per line to sum up my husband's life. I toiled over this task for quite a while. How do you do justice to summing up someone's life in 45 characters? I think I came close. Husband, father, friend, and physician were the roles in life that mattered most to Jeff. I wish I could've added beloved grandfather, brother, and uncle, too. What was important to Jeff was connecting meaningfully with people and living life on his own terms. That is a life well lived.

Section 2:
What Does Grief Feel Like?

Everyone experiences grief differently. It's easy to agree with this statement, but more complex to understand why. Who you are as a person, what your relationship was like with your loved one, and the nature of your current family and living circumstances are just some factors that differentiate individual responses. Even under similar circumstances, what people feel on the inside and show on the outside are often different. The more internal responses differ from outward behavior, the more distress a bereaved person may feel. Maintaining a façade of being fine when you're not is exhausting; I tried to avoid that. In the following pages, I've written about how my grief made me feel. Some of those feelings may strike a chord with you. You might think that I've overlooked an important emotion you've experienced or are facing now. If so, I hope it encourages you to continue exploring your feelings and reflecting on how you're moving through your grief.

Grief Makes You Weary

Grief is an overpowering experience affecting mind, body, and soul. Initially, there's such a pervasive sense of being overwhelmed that just getting out of bed, eating, and showering are major accomplishments. The profound shock and devastation over losing Jeff so suddenly produced physical feelings and sensations with a depth and breadth I still find truly indescribable. Sometimes, the weight felt crushing, morphing into a sense of being hollowed out, shaved off millimeter by millimeter. Often, it was a discomfort felt over my heart. I would, at times, look down at my chest expecting to find a large hole had burned through my sternum directly into my heart—thus the origin of the term heartache. Yet, right after someone dies, particularly when it's a sudden death, it seems like 25 decisions must be made in the first 48 hours. If you haven't made plans for your loved one's death, you'll face an additional glut of unforeseen, energy-draining situations. Anguish and reality collide to exhaust you in every imaginable way.

Grief and loss carry a solidity that presses into you—the air feels thinner, your thoughts less sharp, your spirit diminished. Sometimes, grief is a lump of coal buried in your pocket. If you feel for it, it's always there, dark and dense. Other times, it's a 100-pound boulder on your back, yet capable of radiating heat and light through the gift of memory. As time has passed, my grief has not incapacitated me, but a weight still rests on my shoulders. It's a challenge to find a lightness of being again.

Support from family and friends was crucial right after Jeff died. The kids listened to me and let me cry and tell endless dad stories. My daughter stayed with me the week after Jeff died and made sure I ate. I was surprised by how well I slept, but in retrospect, I was so exhausted from grieving that I collapsed into bed each night, completely worn out, wishing to think and feel nothing. After that, I had to curate my days with what activities I thought I could accomplish. Some days, I was remarkably productive, others not so much. I allowed myself to rest and embraced the relief of quietude whenever I needed a slower pace and less clamor.

It's markedly different for me to be more measured, as opposed to feeling driven to accomplish more than a full day's worth of activities during my waking hours. While I can push myself if needed, I generally move forward with more moderate expectations now. I'm not the same person I was. Sometimes that's a good thing.

I was aware of another sense of my inner self before Jeff's death, but his passing brought it back to me fully. The other time in my life when I became physically and emotionally depleted was during the divorce from my first husband. After all was said and done, and the divorce process was finalized, I became aware that my emotional reservoir had been partially but permanently depleted.

What do I mean by emotional reservoir? All of the angst of going through the process of divorce, and the emotional exhaustion that accompanies it, had taken an unseen piece out of me—a deep wound that eventually heals but leaves a hidden scar. The experience of divorce had laid bare the vulnerability of love, and when circumstances spiral miserably out of control, profound emotional pain and weariness follow.

When you're young, in love, and haven't experienced emotional trauma earlier in life, you don't just throw caution to the wind—you have no caution. You and your partner believe now is forever and nothing will change. Your passion will endure for a lifetime, and it's invincible, just like the two of you. Youth can be incredibly bittersweet in its naivety.

    I thank my lucky stars my emotional reservoir was high enough to let Jeff into my life. I let him in fully, and he enriched my life in ways I couldn't have imagined; it was the best decision I've ever made. But, as I was reminded by Jeff's passing, with great love comes great anguish when that person no longer physically exists in your life. Curating your emotional life—deciding what risks to take and where to tread more carefully—requires introspection, self-awareness, and an understanding of how a traumatic event, like the death of a loved one, has changed you.

    Over the years of being married to Jeff, I realized my emotional reservoir had receded, and I'd become careful about how I engaged in relationships with friends and family. I talked to Jeff about my seemingly decreased ability to tolerate emotional pain, and he understood. His understanding came not only from his professional training and clinical experience, but also from having lived long enough to experience it himself.

    When I had a falling out with a close friend and was deeply hurt by her actions, I wanted to have a frank conversation and confront her. My emotions were running high because I truly cared about this person. I told Jeff about my intention and he strongly advised me against it. I was taken aback. Knowing the details of my relationship with this friend, Jeff believed no conversation we might have could repair or restore it to what it had been. He also knew I would only be hurt further by looking for responses I would never get. He needed to ask me several times what I hoped would be accomplished in this conversation and whether it would satisfy me. I finally agreed not to initiate a conversation with her. Over time, I came to see Jeff was right. It was one of those situations where, after running headfirst into a brick wall several times, you finally stop, realizing you have a choice to end the self-inflicted pain.

Emotional and financial investments have much in common; both involve risk and reward. You can become rich beyond measure if you make the "right" investment emotionally or financially, just in very different ways. Make a poor decision and you become depleted—you're tapped out. Did you learn anything from the misadventure? Do you make the same poor decision again? Do you pick yourself up, wiser than you were, and stride more carefully into the next decision?

It's been a year and a half since Jeff passed. I feel secure in my sense of who I am, even as I search for how I'll live the rest of my life. Being comfortable in my own skin allows me to experience others more empathically. I'm less swift to judge, but more certain to act according to what I believe is true. I'm not sure I can explain exactly why I feel this way, other than writing a book like this makes you reflect a lot. Tomorrow, my world could be turned upside down and everything could change. I can't predict how I'll react or what I'll do then, but I'm hoping to remember everything I've just written.

A Visit from Guilt

At times, grief seems to have an unpleasant companion, guilt. And guilt came for a visit within a couple of months of Jeff's passing. I felt like I'd established a foothold, an internal commitment, to move forward, but the sense of grief was simply overwhelming. I tried to remind myself that progress toward establishing a different life without my loving partner could occur with his memory still fully present. Yet somehow, guilt whispered that moving forward and making progress meant forsaking the memory of my loved one.

Initially, I tried so hard to feel grateful for the good life I shared with Jeff. But gratitude isn't something you can talk yourself into when you're heartbroken and realize nothing will ever be the same again. And, it won't. It's a tough juxtaposition to "move forward"—whatever that means for you—and genuinely feel some comfort and peace from recalling that most special relationship.

Other types of thoughts stealthily creep in after your loved one dies, asking questions to which the answers can never be changed. The exam has already been turned in to the professor—too late to alter any responses; the final grade has been posted. The outcome, death, cannot be changed, yet all sorts of second-guesses filter into one's consciousness. Should I have let Jeff enjoy more of his guilty pleasures instead of trying to feed him healthier food choices? Jeff loved red meat, butter, sausage pizza, and many other tasty pleasures that didn't often find their way onto his dinner plate. What real difference would it have made? I don't know if eating healthier added one day to his life. I'll never know and perhaps it's better that way.

In my head, I've reviewed the circumstances of Jeff's death countless times: what happened in the hours before we went to bed, every action I took after waking up to find him unresponsive, and every emotion I felt. Might I have saved him if I'd woken up in the middle of the night? It is a gut-wrenching process because I can change none of it. I have come to the conclusion I did the best I could. I would've given my life for his, taken his failing heart and handed him mine, but that wasn't a choice granted to me. In virtual conversations with myself and a higher power, I've been clear-eyed in this resolve—I would have traded my life for Jeff's in a heartbeat. I've never wavered from that thought; I would've readily given my life for his. But there's a problem with that line of reasoning. If in some magical universe it was possible to change places, then Jeff would be left to grieve, feel the pain of deep loss, and have to create a different life.

This dilemma is obscurely and classically termed a "Cornelian choice," where either outcome in a tough situation is problematic and less than desirable. I internally wrestled with this conflict for a while. Jeff had, what I can only assume to be, a swift and relatively painless death. But he enjoyed life, and his was cut too short. His loss shattered my world, but I get to live. Ultimately, I must accept things for the way they are, and I do.

I've come to terms with my Cornelian choice, and my reasoning goes like this: I cannot endure the thought Jeff would have to suffer if I'd been the one to die first. If I truly loved him, then I need to take the hit for all the emotional pain and life changes that come with this loss. Maybe he would've done just fine without me—I'll never know. An implicit understanding with your partner is that you'll protect and take care of each other. There are no good options here, but I can't bear the idea of Jeff having to go through this.

You may wonder, what's the point of engaging in this thought process? If I can't change the outcome, why tread into these perilous waters? I don't think I'm the first person, nor will I be the last, to have the heartfelt desire to trade places with their lost loved one. There's survivor guilt when you genuinely would've traded places. I don't believe my resolution of this conflict is a trick of the mind. Grieving is hard and the depths of sorrow are unknown until you have to go through it. Though I didn't get to choose, my choice is to take the hit.

I'm not alone among grievers in having a sense of guilt over some aspect of my loved one's living and dying. Jeff loved me deeply, and he put up with my attempts to get him to adopt healthier life habits. He also didn't let me get away with being outrageous or wallowing in my convoluted thinking. Jeff had an honest and direct approach to dealing with whatever came his way; guilt and regret were not part of his equation.

But my words weep loudly as I write them, and salty tears crystalize on the page. What might Jeff tell me now to try and ease my pain? "Lisa, I love you, don't cry for me so much—a little is okay," he would say with a wry smile. "You did the best you could. I always knew you loved me, and that was what mattered most, so stop crying while you write this."

As the months have passed since Jeff's death, I've heeded my husband's advice, and guilt hasn't been a frequent visitor. Jeff was my biggest fan, and he was all about helping people, including me, progress to the next developmental phase in the best way possible. My heart aches with his memory, as his words of encouragement echo in my ears.

"*I Am Shattered*"

That was my answer when people asked how I was doing right after Jeff died. Honest and succinct. They asked—I didn't lie or gloss it over. I felt like a fluorescent bulb unceremoniously dropped to the floor; burning bright one minute, then splintered into a million pieces the next. I didn't have the capacity at that point to give a nuanced response or reassure the person who asked that, somehow, I wasn't in agony. Some people, even before I could answer, took the question back, feeling embarrassed for having asked it. They quickly realized I couldn't feel anything but completely devastated.

Now, a few months after Jeff's death, when people ask, "How are you doing?"—in that very specific way indicating they want to know how I'm coping with his death—I say, "Okay." That "okay" is spoken in a subdued tone. Tone communicates a great deal to the person who asked the question. Most people get the idea and don't say, "I'm so glad you're doing well." At that point, I shift the focus to them and ask, "How are your children doing? Your wife? Your dog?" Then the conversation moves on.

The first New Year after Jeff passed away, a good friend asked how my New Year's was. I half-laughed and said, "Ask me another question." She did. My honest answer to her original question would've been, "Well, pretty shitty since it occurred to me I could look forward to a whole year without the man I adored." I chose another route to direct the conversation. I won't create a cover story about what's happening to me or how I feel; that's draining and doesn't allow me to be true to myself. But I don't need to lay out every thought running through my head either. That can be taxing, too.

There's an internal repair process that takes place while grieving, your body and soul trying to glue and stitch all those fragments of light back together. But there are seams, some discernable and others invisible. And you can't find all the pieces; some have gone missing. It takes a lot of energy to do this work, so I choose my context wisely—sharing when it feels right and having a scripted response when it doesn't. When a friend truly asks how I'm doing and I want to share, I do. Most importantly, I must remain authentic to my inner sense of self.

***

Time has passed, and it's about a year and a half since Jeff died. I've become very aware of who I can share certain thoughts with about my internal process of bereavement. I now have a body of experience voicing to others the details, depth, and breadth of acute grief and the aftermath of living with profound loss. Those folks who deeply loved their lost one, members of this unfortunate club, have no trouble understanding "feeling untethered from the world" or bursting into tears when a summons for jury duty arrives in the mail—not for you, but for your loved one—who will never have to trudge to the county courthouse again to meet their civic responsibility.

I try to choose carefully who I share with, but sometimes I make a mistake. The person may not have experienced anything that truly allows them to comprehend my feelings or the depth of my loss, but they believe they do. Some response of presumed understanding will follow, and then I resent it. That was my mistake in making a rash decision to share a thought or feeling the moment it popped into my head. Maybe I was tired or needed to relieve the tension the issue

Adventure on Joyland Road

triggered. But friends don't like to hear they can't understand something just because they haven't experienced it; mostly, they want to help. For others, their commiseration may be a chance to demonstrate the breadth of their knowledge and understanding of the world and its miseries. It's an awkward moment and I try to escape as gracefully as possible. Afterward, I need to revisit those situations and learn from them.

As for my current answer to the question, "How are you?" I still mostly respond with "Okay," "All right," or the occasional, "Good." Okay was generally my baseline response before Jeff died and remains so now. I have a widower neighbor, Carl, who, when asked the simple greeting "How are you?" answers without fail, "Fantastic" or "Awesome." I admire that; it's not a flip response. I believe Carl means it, as it reveals the deliberate way he chooses to live that day. In trying to put themselves back together, people find all sorts of ways—authentic ways—to create their own light. When others see and feel that optimism and energy, it creates a warm, welcoming presence that reflects back to its source.

Note to self: There is much to learn from others like Carl. Their actions and their truth may not be exactly right for me, but it's worth scrutinizing to see how it works. It's like trying on a new style of clothing I never thought would fit, but surprisingly, it's more comfortable than I thought. I might end up wearing it or maybe I won't, but at least I gave it a shot.

Dancing with Grief

Early on, to counteract the intense grief, there was a good deal of self-talk that went on inside my head. "I have the skills to move forward, that's what I must do." I said that a lot to myself. On the bereavement merry-go-round, I kept grasping for the brass ring of hope, trying to believe I could get through this grim ride. Could I find a way to talk myself into feeling less lousy?

A friend once told me a good marriage can be like a "finishing school"; that is, a way to learn how to be a better person as an individual and a better person in a relationship. I credit Jeff with creating that kind of environment in our marriage. So, can't my "better self" find a way to improve my mood, look on the bright side, and find something positive to hang onto? If I can't, won't I be forsaking his memory? This may not be the debate-winning argument I was looking for, as an element of guilt is baked in, but it's an explanation still worthy of further examination.

Perhaps I'm overthinking my emotional state and putting too much pressure on myself, but I entered this situation and the ensuing grief as who I am. This is the hand I have to play. I try to use coping strategies that work and discard those that don't. This requires honest, ongoing self-reflection and sharing with trusted others so I can hear myself think out loud. If I'm being too hard on myself, perhaps someone else can bring it into the light so I can take a closer look.

One of the tried-and-true coping strategies I've always relied on

Adventure on Joyland Road

is the mantra, "Things could always be worse." "The hurricane only destroyed half the house, it could've been worse. I only fractured my arm when I fell off the cliff, that could've been a lot worse." There's always some silver lining if you just look hard enough. The silver lining strategy serves as an antidote to self-pity, which can be a distraction when you're looking to move forward in a positive way. In *The Year of Magical Thinking*, Joan Didion wrote, "I just can't see the upside in this," referring to her husband's sudden death from a cardiac arrest. She too, "had been someone who could look for, and find, the upside in any situation." But, not this one. Me either, Joan Didion, me either.

This grieving process can take a while, moving at its own inexplicable pace. Living with wearisome emotional pain and moving forward are not separated by time and space; pain and progress occur in tandem. These fraternal twins couldn't be more different, yet they were birthed from the same tragedy. Common wisdom says being stressed or challenged by life's circumstances often propels us to a higher level of functioning. Perhaps so, but I definitely could've lived without this one.

Grief feels like a constant push-pull battle of trying to make progress, only to get swallowed up in the mind's quicksand of facing another day without the person I called the light of my life. So, I try to think of what Jeff would want for me. I believe he wants the best for me, not to suffer, to care for myself, and find happiness. It's a struggle to find a balance. Alongside that mental scuffle, I carry with me all the skills I learned from living with Jeff, which have made me a more capable person. Yes, I entered the marriage with a certain resilient, never-say-die attitude. But now, in this disequilibrium of grieving his absence every minute, I don't want to let him down—I want him to be proud of me.

I find the thought of wanting Jeff to be proud of me puzzling. I'm a grown adult and senior citizen by U.S. standards. Why would I want my dead spouse to be proud of me? This isn't easy for me to unravel. Looking through the rear-view mirror, I feel like I came into our marriage in need of further emotional development, though I couldn't see it then. Jeff was more patient and forgiving than me, less quick to flare, and deeply honest with himself and others.

Jeff was such an astute psychiatrist that my failings had to be almost immediately visible to him, yet he loved me nonetheless. Over the years of our marriage, we never went to bed mad. Maybe we had a bad minute or bad hour, but we never had a bad day. As upset as I might've been about something, he would never let me walk away angry and isolate myself, no storming out of the house in a frenzy. He would find a way for us to talk the problem through and come to some resolution—no bricks in the wall.

That's a problem for some marriages, those unresolved issues over the years when hurtful things are said and done. They are bricks laid down one at a time until, finally, two people have built an entire wall between them. Jeff didn't let that happen. He was incredibly generous in often being the "bigger person" by toning down the emotions when we disagreed, offering what he might've done differently, and, without saying it out loud, role-modeling how I could behave reciprocally. We both would apologize if we had raised our voices. And I slowly learned to be more patient, that I wasn't right all the time, and to stay calm in the face of adversity. I began to see my words and actions from a point of view other than mine. I could say I was sorry more easily and actually mean it.

There was also another side to Jeff that surprised me at first. He didn't flinch when a conflict arose, and most people were no match for his quick thinking and verbal skills. Jeff wasn't physically imposing; the odds weren't high that he would win a fistfight. But he didn't take shit from anybody, and he was quick to recognize and respond when it came his way—even if he was just a bystander to excrement floating past. When I first saw this behavior, I was floored.

Adventure on Joyland Road

We were standing in a grocery store waiting to check out. A customer in front of us was verbally abusive to the checkout clerk. Jeff looked at the customer and firmly uttered one word: "Stop!" The man he spoke to turned and briefly looked at Jeff, surprise registering on his face at being called out for his bad behavior. The man stopped, and without saying another word, left the store. My jaw dropped. The clerk said some kind words to Jeff, mentioning upset customers were part of her day, but I could see she was touched.

I saw Jeff do this several times during our marriage. Sometimes it happened with strangers; other times, with family, where the emotional stakes were much higher. Jeff would not allow others to disrespect or humiliate him, and he would draw a line in the sand. Deciding to address an act of disrespect can carry consequences, but I guess it comes down to this, if you can't respect yourself, why should anyone else? So, besides learning to be more patient, Jeff taught me to be less fearful of confrontation. Standing up for yourself and others can be a learned skill, and I got to see firsthand how it was done.

Jeff also taught me the art of quickly understanding the motivations of others and how they might play out in my interactions with them. Words and behaviors all carry meaning, it's just a matter of piecing together what that meaning is. In my professional life, this valuable skill helped me immeasurably to navigate bureaucratic waters, understand the hidden agenda behind the public one, and chart the best course forward. Let me give you an example.

The first dean I worked for, Dr. Kim Alexander, was a lovely human being. She didn't have a mean bone in her body, and if someone did her wrong, she didn't carry a grudge. Several candidates had vied for the coveted position of dean of the college, but Dr. Alexander got the job. Another candidate, Leslie, had been with the organization for many years and thought she was in line for the deanship; Kim, an outsider, got the job instead. Leslie continued her employment in another department of the organization and moved up through the ranks.

Whenever Kim tried to work on joint ventures with Leslie, there always seemed to be resistance or opposition. One day, Kim bemoaned how Leslie was difficult to work with and outright dismissive at times. I exclaimed to her, "Leslie behaves this way because you got the job she thought she had a right to. It isn't you personally, Kim, that she dislikes. It's the fact that it was you instead of her who was chosen to be dean." Kim looked at me and said, "You think that's it?" I firmly responded, "Yes, I do." From then on, Kim saw me differently—as someone who could advise her on how best to approach matters when interpersonal issues were at play, an *eminence grise*, if you will. I continued to use that skill throughout my professional career.

Finding meaning in this life I've been unexpectedly given is perhaps the most critical driving force behind my desire to be someone Jeff would be proud of. There's unfinished business left regarding the children and grandchildren. Jeff never stopped being a parent, grandparent, brother, and uncle—not for a minute. He wholly embraced his role as the paterfamilias. His approach was generous and fearless as he listened and counseled his family. I cannot count the number of times I have heard family say, "Boy, I wish Jeff were here to talk to right now." Yup, I say that a lot, too.

I understand I can't be Jeff, nor do I try to be. But as I tangoed with my grief over the months, I learned some things along the way—like how important it is to be there for people, truly listen, and provide support. I adopted Jeff's outlook that your kids, no matter how old, still need a parent to love and comfort them, as well as someone to talk to. Grandkids need a doting grandparent who loves them unconditionally, yet someone they also can talk to about anything. I can't be Jeff, but I can be the me that has evolved, the one I hope he would be proud of.

Aren't I Supposed to Be Feeling Better by Now?

This hard-to-admit-to-myself thought occurred to me several months after Jeff had passed away. Why is it hard to admit? Wasn't I supposed to feel less burdened by grief, at least just a little? Two weeks after Jeff died, I got teary in front of one of Jeff's friends, Wayne, who seemed caught off guard by my emotionality. He said impulsively, "You've got to get over this." I remember looking at him and mumbling it was so hard not having Jeff standing next to me—living, breathing, laughing—and how much I loved him. Wayne quickly retreated from his comment and invited me to stay at his and his wife's home for a while. I didn't take him up on his offer, heartfelt and genuine as it might've been.

Friends and family are doing their best to be supportive, but it seems unless they've been through a devastating loss, it's difficult to understand the magnitude. You don't want people to know this pain, but if they have a great love in their life, they inevitably will. I'm deeply sorry for the penetrating sense of loss they'll encounter. When you have no measure for the depth and breadth of the experience, finding the right words to offer comfort can be difficult.

Almost everyone who hasn't experienced a sudden, catastrophic loss has some anxiety about it. The reality of "here one day and gone the next" is hard for people to process. They might understand it feels bad, even overwhelming, but they can't truly grasp what this beast is, so they project their anxiety onto you. Though I recognize these attempts are well-meaning, thankfully, I haven't been inundated with comments like, "You're such a strong woman," "I understand how you feel," or "Don't worry, you'll get over it." That would've been hard to bear.

People have said with some frequency, "At least he didn't suffer." I can't tell you if he did or didn't. I was asleep next to him when the fatal event occurred; I perceived nothing and didn't wake. I also have heard, "At least you had him for the time you did" or some variant. Well, he isn't here now, and there's never enough time. If I'm in a particularly off mood when this is said to me, I imagine the person's next sentence is, "So just be grateful and move on." When these comments come my way, I remind myself they aren't about me, but the other person searching for the silver lining in my grief. Joan Didion rings in my head—there is no upside to be found here.

I believe most people have good intentions; they're trying their best to help. As a supportive friend or family member, aren't you supposed to help the aggrieved feel better? The unintended consequence of those well-meaning comments is they shut down any further meaningful exchange. Whatever way I might wish to explain my pain or state of mind, I find myself blocked. Pain is hard to listen to. Simply being present is enough, but that's not easy to do either; silence can feel uncomfortable.

And what does it even mean to be present? There aren't any prescribed things you do or say to be empathically present for another human being. The best way I can describe being present in this situation is to fully engage with the other person in the moment, deeply listen, and reflect on what the grieving person shares. By meeting someone where they are in their journey—not where you think or hope they should be—you affirm for the aggrieved that it's okay to be just where they are and feel what they feel. Most people want you to embrace gratitude, hoping it will mitigate some of the anguish of grief. Don't get me wrong, I'm a big fan of gratitude. But gratitude is a personal reconciliation reached, understood, and integrated through private reflection.

One morning a personal encounter with gratitude occurred when I was taking a 7 AM swim outdoors. At that time of the day, I'm alone in the pool and find the exercise and breathing of swimming meditative. A sliver of the moon was still in the morning sky, and the wind was mild. I could hear the leaves moving gently with the breeze as the robins and sparrows sang their early morning secret songs. At that moment, an epiphany hit me—compared to the more horrific end-of-life circumstances I've seen other loved ones go through, I was grateful Jeff's sudden death wasn't stricken with intense suffering. It was something I didn't just think but felt.

When someone else tells you to be grateful for the circumstances of your loved one's death, at best, it doesn't work; at worst, it makes you feel bad, as though you should be doing a better job grieving. You're the only one taking this trip—you're the driver, the navigator, and the unwilling passenger. Everybody wants to give you directions, those who have gone down this road and those who have not, but it's singularly your journey. There's no Google map to guide you, telling you to turn right in 450 feet, and you'll find a gas station on the corner to refill your tank. You don't have to rush to a destination when the road to get there is still unclear. Right now, I don't exactly know where I'm supposed to be going.

A close friend, Kate, who lost her husband three months before Jeff passed away, told me about her encounter with Anna, a widow from Eastern Europe who was visiting the U.S. My friend was inundated more than I was with people telling her, in one way or another, to get past her grief. Anna, who'd been widowed for 12 years, was unapologetic about the nature of her grief. Her heartache was still present, and Anna had no hesitation in talking about it. At times, Anna's openness made others uncomfortable, but my friend found it refreshingly honest and freeing. Kate is ultra-smart, capable, and psychologically perceptive, but even she needed permission to simply be—to feel unapologetic about giving voice to her true feelings. I've come to understand this sense of loss may never leave me, but it's not abnormal; it's not something to be fixed or feel guilty about because it lingers in my consciousness. I'm letting life unfold before me without judgment, from myself or others. It is what it is.

Who Am I?

How do I define who I am? What is my social identity? Nurse, educator, sports lover, friend, mother, grandmother, spouse? One of those identities suddenly dropped off the list and changed from spouse to widow. That change in social identity is a jolt to the psyche. Whatever emotional attachment I had to identify as a "wife" or "spouse" just went out the window.

Widows and widowers sometimes say to the newly widowed, "You just became a member of a club you didn't want to join." A big part of how I saw myself, a role I gladly occupied in life, no longer exists; a spouse is what I was. In objective terms, how society defines me—as a widow—is the checkbox choice. There it is in black and white, right on the form I have to sign. I am now defined as a widow. It's a shock to the system.

Though I've made it my mission to stay calm, as there isn't much that should annoy me now in the grand scheme of things, this does. It's even more vexing when only two choices are provided—married and single. Excuse me? Please don't try to talk sense to me and say whoever is asking this question is only trying to find out my current marital status. I've been married since I was 20 years old until I was 68, except for the two intervening years between my husbands. I didn't get unmarried to Jeff; he died. At least the widowhood checkbox acknowledges a past life I hold so deeply dear.

Some of these ubiquitous forms have found a way to be more inclusive of gender identity, offering options beyond the binary choice of male and female. Even then, many non-cisgender people find the options inadequate. But these square, little marital status boxes seemingly scream at you to conform—to contort yourself into a shape that's so distorted from explaining your existence and who you really are. I want to scream back, "I'm a person who lost my beloved spouse after 30 years of our being together. It hurts beyond measure. I hate having to answer this question, but you put one of those little asterisks by it, so a response is required. Now, you force me into this checkmark of reality. Thanks a lot for the uninvited reminder."

This sense of loss of identity is like having a phantom limb. That appendage, which used to be a part of me, giving me stability and helping define who I was in life, is suddenly gone—precipitously amputated. It's a different sensation than the pain of grief; it's a distortion of my internal image, a disfigurement only I can see.

My tangible, living and breathing, beloved Jeff is gone, but so is a chunk of my outward, social identity. It takes a lot of getting used to. I dislike having to redefine myself as a widow, but that's what I've become. It's a bad-fitting prosthetic, and I don't know how to wear it.

My wedding ring is a gold band with two rows of small diamonds, each column separated by a gold strip. I still wear it on my real left hand. It is a phantom reality, but one I can't let go of. I've tried putting the ring on my right hand, but my left fourth finger feels naked and vulnerable. If I ever decide to change, I know I'll experience some uneasiness for a while.

I see a goodly number of widows wearing their wedding rings as well. It's a hard-to-break attachment. Each morning your spouse woke up next to you—an everyday occurrence that, before they died, could easily be taken for granted. Slipping on a wedding ring every day was just one more movement, that through sheer repetition, became almost unconscious. Wearing my wedding ring now is a deeply conscious and defining act—a declaration of who I was and still am. It's a testament to the great love we shared, even though the outward manifestation, Jeff in the flesh, no longer exists.

I noted to a widowed friend that some women continue to wear their wedding rings, and others don't. Over dinner together, I asked her why she still wore hers. She looked down at her left fourth finger and said her wedding ring reminded her of her husband and their relationship. Wearing it made her feel better. It doesn't need to get more complicated than that.

Some friends and acquaintances struggle to adjust to your new identity when one day you're married, and the next, you're widowed. People knew and engaged with you and your spouse in one fixed way, and then suddenly, you alone are thrust into an unforeseen next phase in your life. Some couples may stay socially engaged with you in your new single status (bless you, folks). Sometimes, these relationships change; married friends may call you less or make fewer, if any, social engagements with you as a single person. For some friends who hadn't consciously considered that one day they, too, might be traveling down this road, one's mere presence—minus your spouse—may give rise to a sense of discomfort and questions they would rather not know the answers to. I'm clear about one thing: the anxiety they feel emanates from them, not me. It's their issue.

Our life experiences continue to alter how we define ourselves and our subsequent social identities. I might make a different decision tomorrow based on what happens today and a renewed understanding of myself. It's all a work in progress. And I mean progress in two ways: the work is unfinished, but it's a moving forward not a regression, even if at times it feels like two steps forward and one step back. That is my mindset. There's no other choice I'll entertain.

Section 3:
Memories

Memories are the double-edged sword of loss—sometimes it's hard to live with them and, other times, you can't go on without them. And that's what makes them so complicated. It's worth examining how memories operate when you're grieving; otherwise, you risk being constantly blown about by unexpected winds of emotion. It will still happen anyway, but they won't necessarily knock you down. Those who have lost a great love don't describe getting over their loss but living with the presence of their loss. Memories are what that presence is made of.

Walking the Knife's Edge of Memory

It's worth taking a moment to explore how memory works in human beings, as it's a biologically fundamental function essential for survival. Memory, simply put, is the ability to retain information and recall it at a later time. But memories are so much more. They shape our identity—we are who we are because of our memories. Memories guide our thoughts and decisions, and they influence our emotional reactions. The ability to have long-term memories relies on structural changes in our neural networks. What's particularly relevant when people are dealing with grief is that emotionally charged events are better remembered than emotionally neutral experiences, which are often quickly forgotten. Positive (enjoyment and pleasure) or negative (pain, distress, trauma) emotions can help consolidate the recollection of a memory. It's no wonder that memories are everywhere when you're grieving. They're so easily resurrected when two lives are closely entwined over so many years; they can't be avoided. I came to understand this soon after Jeff died, when a daily barrage of memories was triggered by, well, everything.

There's a difference between the memories I call up in conversations with people and ones that pop in uninvited. It wasn't uncommon for me early on, and still isn't, to recall a memory of Jeff or an experience we had and bring that up at an appropriate moment in a conversation. I find that to be a positive experience—no wonder.

Adventure on Joyland Road

I have some control in bringing Jeff to life for a fleeting instant in a more comforting, nostalgic way. I can soothe myself recalling how he used to kiss my forehead tenderly (I called them "angel kisses"), how soft to the touch his beard was, or the fineness of his hair.

But the appearance of surprising, uninvited memories can leave me unsettled, unnerved, trembling, or outright weeping. And those damn triggers are everywhere. They're in Diet Coke and pistachio ice cream as I pass them in the grocery store; seeing a St. Bernard on the street (because Murray, the 99-lb. runt St. Bernard Jeff owned, was his favorite dog); or hearing any love song that reminds me of Jeff. It's an echo chamber of memories that reverberates with the sights, sounds, and stories of our past.

I thought those disturbing reactions would lessen over the months, but not so much—triggers aren't predictable. If you've chosen to acknowledge and experience your grief, to let it walk with you as you try to find the resolve to keep moving forward, then triggers are going to happen. I don't perceive myself as being constantly ignited by the flame of memory and reduced to wallowing in the ashes of grief and negativity. I try to live a purposeful life, socially and professionally, though I'm still finding my way. Yet, there they are, embers of memories flickering in the shadows.

The unexpected appearance of memories can be disconcerting. "You see me, I know you do. Deal with me now," they say. As I see it, there are three reactions or choices when unanticipated memories arise. You can:

1) Ignore these uninvited visitors and let them drift back down into some unconscious place. This tactic doesn't work. Memories are like ghosts that rise and filter back into consciousness. It's like ignoring water that begins to enter a leaky boat—wait too long, and you'll end up swimming for your life. It's better to bail some out, see where the leak is coming from, and address it. I might spring another leak

somewhere else, but at least I won't end up sinking under the weight of all that emotional water.

2) Acknowledge the memory and sadness that wells up, as it's all that remains in the unending absence of my loved one. Tears almost inevitably follow, and I search for ways to comfort myself back to baseline functioning

3) Respond to the memory and the experience that triggered it with gratefulness.

I confess to doing all three. I wish I could do more of choice three, but it isn't easy. There's a residue of sadness that exists after a loved one dies, making despondency (choice 2) the more automatic, go-to response early in the grief process. It's why gratitude as a life philosophy is so important. I feel gratitude in so many ways toward my posse of family and friends, however, feeling grateful when a memory of Jeff is aroused is often harder to summon. Adjusting to ever-present reminders and recollections is an entirely internal process. Memories can be a tricky balancing act of feeling sadness and solace simultaneously. It's sometimes hard to predict how it will play out. But I am sure of one thing—the experiences I have moving forward without him will continue to remind me of the experiences we shared as a couple.

A large photo of Jeff hangs in our hallway along with several other family photographs. A friend took this particular photo of Jeff, capturing his piercing blue eyes and the slightest of wry smiles. When friends and family see this photo, they say it embodies Jeff's essence. I think so too, and every time I pass it in the hallway, that thought runs through my head. Over the months, the photo became, at times, more painful to look at; it made me ache for Jeff, and I'd look away from it as I passed through the hallway. And, then, more than a year and a half after his death, I walked up to the photo and looked at it closely—but somehow differently—and realized this was Jeff's,

"Here's looking at you, kid. You know, I love you" expression.

The phrase, "Here's looking at you, kid," is the famous Humphrey Bogart line said to Ingrid Bergman at the end of the iconic movie, Casablanca. Their characters, Rick and Lisa, love each other, but a future together is not to be. The "look" Rick gives Lisa must last forever. Jeff would've liked being compared to Bogart in Casablanca—a tough, quiet guy who didn't complain and acted selflessly, even if it came at a deep personal cost. My external eyes and internal lens found a way to have a different perspective on Jeff's photo and gratitude for the expression I now see.

Another image also comes to mind when I look at Jeff's photo. The projector reel spins in my head, like one of those old black-and-white movies in which a young man, smitten and in love, must say goodbye to his lover at the train station. As the train slowly begins to creep out of the station, the young man runs after the train and jumps on the train stairs, his lover standing just behind the closed door. The lovers hold their hands to the breath-steamed window for a few seconds, fingers outstretched on the impenetrable pane of glass that separates them, until the young man must jump off the train. He can't go with his lover—at least not now. This is not a train for which he can buy a ticket. But while he waits for the time when they may be reunited, that one enduring moment is etched forever in the outline of his hand.

***

The story below, The Last Hurrah, is one I recall with a bittersweet feeling. It's a memory that touches my soul in ways few other stories do.

The Last Hurrah

In the preceding months before Jeff passed away, we decided to do some home remodeling. After living in our condominium for 20 years, we'd made a few updates here and there—but not many. We had already replaced some carpeting with wood floors, and honestly, the remaining carpet was well past its prime. Jeff was a wood guy, so we decided it was time to replace the rest. The only problem was the existing wood flooring would need to be sanded and stained to match the new flooring. That would require Jeff and I to move ourselves and the furniture out of the apartment for some time.

If you've ever remodeled your home, you can envision what's coming next. As long as Jeff and I and the furniture had to go, wasn't this a good time to paint the walls? But, wait, let's not stop there. Since the clothes needed to be removed from the closets, why not re-do them and ditch the builder's grade wire racks? And, at the last minute, our shades were starting to show their age, so let's replace them, too. When all was said and done, the scope of the work would require us to vacate our home for about a month. Jeff was none too pleased. Before the work began, we had to pack countless boxes with our belongings, disassemble complicated electronics, and hire another company to dismantle the modular office furniture in our study.

I had a recommendation for a general contractor from one of our neighbors. Though Jeff and I had little experience of late doing home remodeling, we both felt we were a pretty good judge of character. Rick, a wiry man in his 40s, came to our home and assessed the work we wanted done. He had flooring and painting sub-contractors he thought would be the right match for our projects. Rick was personable and seemed knowledgeable and honest; we liked him. He sent us a proposal and we signed off in October 2021.

We put the work off until January, after the holidays, so I could have ample time to pack us up. I promised Jeff I would pack and unpack every box, and I did. Jeff meticulously labeled every stereo, TV, and computer wire, and disassembled all the electronics. I planned for our stay away at a local residence inn-type setting.

In this remodeling journey, we got to know Rick better. He was a high-energy guy who lived with his young family in a neighboring suburb. Jeff and I liked to get to know the people we hired to work for us, and Jeff was particularly fond of telling stories when they were relevant to the conversation. It didn't matter to either of us this was a person we'd hired to do a job; based on who we were and our professional backgrounds, we engaged with people relationally. Life was rarely a transactional matter for us.

Due to our proactive planning, staying on top of the project as it progressed, Rick's oversight, and good sub-contractors, we moved back into our refreshed home in about three and a half weeks. Amazingly, it all went pretty smoothly. We had a final meeting with Rick, paid him for the rest of the work, and talked about our lives and families.

Several weeks later, Rick called me. He asked if it was okay to talk about one of his children. He knew what Jeff and I had done professionally and said we were the only people with whom he felt comfortable sharing this information. He began to describe some difficulties his young son was having in school and at home. He and his wife had taken their son to his pediatrician who recommended a trial of medication. Though Rick's wife was willing to give the medicine a try, Rick was less convinced. He said he trusted us to give him advice.

I was honored Rick felt he could confide in us and seek counsel. I told him Jeff, not I, was the right person to talk to, as he was the child psychiatrist and had extensive knowledge about the medications. I told Rick I'd talk to Jeff right away, and I did. As soon as I told Jeff what Rick had requested, he asked me to set up a time for Rick to come to our home and meet with him. Jeff also wanted Rick to bring his wife. I called Rick back, and we set a date for him and his wife to come by.

When the date and time arrived for Rick and his wife to visit, I left our apartment and went to our building's hospitality room so the three of them could talk privately. I told Jeff to call me when they were done. Fifty-two minutes later, Jeff called. He said, "I'm done. Apparently, I'm out of practice. It took me 52 minutes instead of 45." I responded, "Don't worry, honey, it was an initial appointment." Jeff replied, "Yeah, you're right. I had to take a history." He treated their visit just like a real appointment he would've conducted in his office!

Jeff provided the advice Rick and his wife were seeking and felt comfortable accepting. Jeff commented afterward on how he had cherished his work and how much he missed it. He loved helping people in the very specialized way he could.

Six weeks later, after that fateful meeting, Jeff passed away. I felt obliged to let Rick know Jeff was no longer with us. This is what I messaged Rick:

> Hi Rick. I know we might not cross paths again in the near future but I felt compelled to let you know that Jeff passed away suddenly last Friday. Not too long ago he said how pleased he was to be able to talk with you and your wife about your son. I wanted to let you know that. My husband truly loved helping people and I hope he was able to do that for your family. Take care.

Shortly after I sent that message, Rick called me. He was shaken and tearful. He told me that based on their conversation with Jeff, he and his wife decided to have their son take the medication recommended by their physician. Rick said his son was doing much better and felt Jeff had changed the course of their family. I was gratified by his words more than I could say. It was Jeff's last act as a psychiatrist—being a helper, a healer. The legacy one leaves by guiding others through life's inevitable challenges creates a powerful ripple effect—touching recipients, their loved ones, and even future generations. Jeff implicitly knew that. He loved being a psychiatrist, specifically the kind of psychiatrist who understood the healing power of the therapeutic relationship.

Adventure on Joyland Road

Note to self: Jeff was a beautiful person, and you were lucky to know him. No, there are never enough memories made to fill the unquenchable thirst for more time. Try to be kind to yourself as you remember the life you shared, and cherish the recollections that have become your keepsakes.

The Small Moments

I always saw life and relationships as a series of moments strung together creating a greater whole. I believe the best of life is lived in these small, unremarkable moments. The bigger events that occur over a lifetime—birthdays, anniversaries, graduations—weren't the defining moments for me or Jeff. It was all the smaller things, like the inside jokes we shared or the physical comedy we both were capable of. When we received a package or box with a gold stretch bow, Jeff would put the bow around his forehead, tilt his head to one side, put his outstretched fingers to his face, and smile as if he were some beatific angel. It cracked me up every time. The incongruity of this pose on a bald, bearded, senior citizen was hilarious. We also relied on reenacting scenes from famous movies for comedic relief, such as in *Young Frankenstein* when the limping Igor leads his guests to their rooms, saying, "Walk this way," and the guests begin limping behind him. In the right context, scenarios like these were always clowning favorites for us.

There are so many changes to reckon with after your loved one dies, not the least of which are the ones to a day's routine—buying groceries, planning social occasions, purchasing a plane ticket, the list goes on and on. All the planning you once did for two is now planning for one, thus, the reminders of the loss are ever-present. It's difficult to forget the patterns of thought and behavior that became ingrained over so many years of sharing your life with someone. And not that you'd necessarily want to.

But sharing the small moments with someone becomes microscopic. Let me illustrate. "How'd you sleep last night, honey? Weren't those blueberries amazing at breakfast? I need to make a dental appointment, that toothache is not going away. Your sister's birthday is tomorrow, we have to remember to call. Did you see my keys? Why don't we call Jim and Cindy and see if they want to join us for dinner this Saturday? Could you rub my shoulders for a minute, they're so tight. Let's work on the taxes tomorrow. What would you like for dinner tonight? Let's stream Professor T's next episode later. Good night, I love you. Love you, too."

That's just a snippet of a day, multiplied by the hundreds of things you say and do with each other. Nothing monumental, but it's the fabric of the relationship. Now add 365 days, times how many years you were together. It embodies a lifetime of moments that no longer exist. I'm not sure feeling the loss of those moments ever leaves, as the triggers for them continue to appear as we live out our lives each day.

Perhaps the most important small moments were the thousands of times we said, "I love you" to each other. Those affirmations were the precious twinkling of bright stars that filled the universe of our relationship. That's what mattered to both of us. It's one way to explain why Jeff is never far from my thoughts.

A response I've gotten from many who have lost their partner or spouse—averting their gaze, as people often do when they're about to give you bad news—is: "It gets easier to bear over time, but it never goes away." Feeling the loss of that person's presence will never go away, not ever. And the first time someone said that to me, it did sound like bad news. This grief was a malady from which I would never recover—a permanent, invisible disability. I'm not sure they meant it that way. They gave me an honest response to the loss of their loved one: that person's day-to-day presence and love were not something they would ever get over. These people weren't debilitated by their loss; they were living with the presence of loss. I understand now.

A Thousand Cuts

The days can be filled with poignant moments, small reminders of how it used to be. I was walking with my good friend, Iris, in late autumn. The sun was shining and the trees were still courageously clinging to their fall color, but the cool temperature portended the winter season. My friend's 84-year-old husband approached us. As the three of us stood and talked, Iris pulled her husband's cap tighter to his ears against the biting wind. She drew him close, gently patted his chest, and kissed him. The wind stung me and brought tears to my eyes, as did her loving gestures, for it's those caring moments I miss so dearly.

Perhaps that's why some widows and widowers fill their social calendars with pleasant distractions, like dinner engagements, attending plays, the opera, or extended vacations—it fends off the inevitable stinging cuts when the mind can roam free, making connections to what is no longer possible. Other widowed spouses quickly seek the company of a new partner, someone with whom they can develop a close and intimate relationship. Everyone's path is different, and people do what they feel they need to move forward. I guess I'm just a plodder and move more slowly. Jeff and I were never in a hurry to fill every spare moment of our lives with social activity. I've retained that same inclination, for better or worse.

Still, sometimes when I see an older couple walking hand-in-hand, a quick wave of jealousy flashes over me. Or if I see a young couple, looking so in love and with all the brightness of their future ahead of them, I am envious. Though I acknowledge these feelings, I don't let them take root. I'm glad others have the eagerness and exhilaration of a new romance. And I wholly appreciate the more enduring love—the kind that acquires a beautiful patina only time and maturity can forge.

But I so want to talk to Jeff, touch his beard, feel his warmth, and tell him everything will be alright. Yes, everything will be okay—that was a thing with us, saying that phrase when nothing else in the psychiatric arsenal would work. Sometimes, when a particularly challenging situation would arise and Jeff was trying to help, I'd look at him and say, "Just tell me, 'Don't worry, honey, everything will be okay'." Jeff would sincerely repeat, "Don't worry, everything will be all right." And I believed him. I now desperately want to say these words to him, to comfort him wherever he is.

The Meaning of Stuff

I live in the same home as we did before Jeff died. All the objects—the "stuff" he touched, things we bought, photos of us—are all there. Reminders are inevitably ever-present. The conundrum of bittersweet recollection is never far away.

Jeff loved black-and-white photography. In particular, he loved the photography of the artist, O. Winston Link, who took photographs of steam engine trains. These photos, painstakingly staged at night with lights to illuminate the surroundings, create just enough contrast and texture to produce marvels of creation. They depict a bygone era of small towns and rural settings. I think Jeff loved them so much because they reminded him of when and where he grew up. The pictures are wonderful in their own right, but the beauty and comfort of memory are embedded in each one. These photos hang in our living room and will until the day I die.

Several historical photographs of Jeff and his family also adorn the walls. Jeff has photos of his father and uncle working in their sign shop, looking seriously into the camera, but just mere boys. There's a large wedding photo of Jeff's parents, his dad in a black tux and white tie, holding a black top hat and white gloves. His mother holds a grand bouquet of white roses and wears an elegant white gown with a flowing train. Jeff's dad has a solemn but contented look. His mother is leaning slightly toward her husband, her smile expressing this is the best day of her life. A colorized baby picture of Jeff hangs in the center of these family photos. He has a pensive look, his eyes gazing into a future he's yet to know. Jeff's vital presence in my life made his past deeply meaningful to me. I'm grounded by these photos.

   Someone asked me early on if I was going to move, as if disposing of the home Jeff and I shared and getting a "fresh start" would be an instant solution to drowning grief. Even contemplating such a move seemed, at best, ill-advised, and at worst, sacrilegious to my husband's memory. Initially, when I looked at Jeff's clothes in the closet, I said, "You can either look at an empty closet or one that still has his stuff in it." I didn't think I could endure passing by an empty closet every day. Objects, photos, clothes, and familiar surroundings still offer the comfort of memory—their presence steadies me. In a way, I feel these tangible objects know me as much as I know them.

   There is one thing I gave away, or I should say, returned, almost immediately after Jeff died. Jeff loved, and I mean seriously loved, Diet Coke. Me, I never touched the stuff. But Jeff could drink copious amounts of that brown liquid and never tire of it. He liked it so much, he never even put it in the fridge or over ice; he just drank it at room temperature. I would buy cartons of Diet Coke or 6-packs, whatever was on sale. I was all in if I could buy four cartons or plastic bottle 6-packs for $12. I'd stock it in our garage storage locker so he'd never run out.

   And then, right after Jeff died, there it all was—six 6-packs of Diet Coke neatly stashed in our wire mesh storage cage, right in front of where I park my car. I don't think it was more than 48 hours after he died when I went down to my car and saw all that Coke sitting there, taunting me: Coke that would never be sipped, guzzled, or enjoyed by Jeff. None of the family drank Diet Coke, I couldn't even give it away. I felt compelled to get rid of it as quickly as possible. I loaded it in my car and drove to the grocery store where I had purchased it. I was in no emotional shape to undertake this self-imposed mission, but I was driven beyond all reason.

Adventure on Joyland Road

Luckily, I knew the store manager, Mark, who was working that day. I approached him and asked if it would be okay to return all the Coke I had recently bought. Mark, a decent and kind man, said, "Of course." And then, unexpectedly, I explained why I wanted to return the Coke. I said my husband had suddenly passed away, and Diet Coke was his favorite beverage. He drank a lot of it, which is why I had purchased so much. I told Mark I couldn't bear to look at it—not in my storage area, on the kitchen table, not anywhere. And, in fact, even now when I pass the large displays of Coke on sale as I enter the grocery store, I turn away. Being in no condition to have this conversation in the first place, I am now openly sobbing in the grocery store. Far from being uncomfortable, Mark was sympathetic and understanding. He took the Coke from me and said he would hug me if it weren't against store policy. I was so grateful for Mark's kindness and not making me feel weird or awkward. I was extremely raw and vulnerable, and he knew just what to say and do.

***

I knew at some point I would have to sell Jeff's car—his silver BMW 435i coupe. Though he might not have favored it as much as some of the other cars he owned, he liked the look and feel of this BMW, and it was comfortable for him to drive. Every day, as I went to my car, I would pass his. I needed to start it from time to time and drive it a little so the battery didn't die. Mostly, it stayed in a resting state, undriven by me and the one who loved cars. The thought of cleaning it out and going through the process of selling it felt completely overwhelming—far beyond anything I could manage in the early going. I'd already paid the insurance for the latest six-month cycle so, in my mind, it was money already spent. It was worth my short-term sanity to let it sit. But I knew that reprieve would only last three months, and then another insurance bill was coming. I tried to steel myself.

About a month before the insurance premium was due, I started to clean out his car. There was lots, and I mean lots of stuff packed into it. The trunk, backseat, console, glovebox, and side panels had towels, baseball caps, a Swiss army knife, a flashlight, road tools, a tollway transponder, service invoices, CDs, a cigar cutter, and so much more crammed into it. The only thing that wasn't in the car was an umbrella, go figure. Once the car was empty, I needed to clean up the interior to make it presentable for sale. I knew it was impossible to do this whole project in one session. It took several trips to the garage to get it done. I dreaded every time I went down there; it felt entirely grim. I would've preferred a root canal.

When I was done with this cheerless project, I needed to figure out where I would sell the car. I settled on CarMax—at least they're efficient. Once I received a price quote from an agent, I had a limited timeframe to sell them the car; otherwise, the offer would expire. That cleaned-out car sat there like a ghost until I set a date to bring it in. I asked my friend, Iris, if she would accompany me, wait while I completed the paperwork, and then drive me home.

As I drove Jeff's car to CarMax that day, I fell apart. This car, an object made of metal and plastic and fabric, still had Jeff's imprint all over it. It was the car we took on a road trip to Kansas City, and the one we drove into downtown Chicago when I would drop him off at his office, go to my workplace, and then pick him up at the end of the day. Jeff was old school enough to invent a small errand just so he could drive around on the weekends. I couldn't shake Jeff's connection to this car and its embodiment of so many memories. When we got to CarMax, Iris saw I was not quite right. I went through the paperwork with the agent, and then it was time for CarMax to take possession of the car. I told my friend I needed to go outside for some air, but I really went outside to cry and say goodbye to the car. I sat in it one last time and told Jeff how sorry I was for selling his car—it was gut-wrenching.

Adventure on Joyland Road

As his silver BMW was slowly driven away from me into the Carmax garage, Iris and I walked to her car. I glanced back one last time before we drove off, knowing this was one more piece of the past that would forever disappear. Iris invited me over for dinner that night, which was a wonderful gesture, and exactly what I needed—to not be alone. The next day when I went down to my car in the garage, there was the empty parking space where the silver BMW had sat the day before. When I returned from my errand, I consciously decided to park in Jeff's spot. I would try that out and see how it felt. And it felt a little better to park there instead of my usual space; like I was occupying a place in this world where Jeff used to be. I did the same thing in our bed. Almost immediately after Jeff died, I started to sleep on his side of the bed. I needed to be where he was.

Many months have passed since I parted with Jeff's car. I still have given away very little of his belongings. At the end of the year, when Jeff and I would usually make our donations to various organizations, I summoned up the determination to take a few items of Jeff's—the black jeans he wore, some oversized sweatshirts, and a few slightly sole-worn shoes—to the local donation center. My logic was these were things my son and son-in-law wouldn't be able to use, which was why I selected these particular garments. But gathering the clothes, taking each item off its hanger, putting them in a plastic bag, and driving them to a new home all felt grave and sorrowful, not liberating. Logic had no utility here. I'm still too cathected to Jeff's things and can't cross that bridge of parting with them. Given some time, I suppose I'll slowly give away more of his clothing to those who need it. But right now, I live in a liminal space between past and present; I'm not ready to give away his personal belongings yet. And that's okay.

My friend, Kate, for a number of reasons, needed to move from her large home into a condominium half the size. What that involved, of course, was donating many items from the home she and her husband, Jack, shared for decades. For Kate, giving away her husband's clothing was not problematic. She did it soon after he died, and Kate easily understood why: Kate associated Jack's clothing with his illness. There weren't any positive memories connected to those bits of cloth and thread.

But when she described what it was like trying to box other items she would have to give away, that was a different story. Jack was an avid reader, and many evenings Kate and Jack would read together in their library. These books—where they were bought, the evenings spent together, and the cards and notes left behind within their pages, only to be discovered on a melancholy day of packing them up—flooded Kate with memories and tears almost to paralysis. She described gathering herself up and pushing on, only to stumble upon another bittersweet memento, tucked away and hidden from the light. This wistful reminder boldly jumps from its secret place, confronting her in this new reality—the one without her husband.

I told Kate not having to move spared me from this agonizing process. I now better understand why I'm so reluctant to give away a stitch of Jeff's wardrobe: his clothing holds positive memories for me. Jeff, most decidedly, didn't like to go clothes shopping (other than Brooks Brothers shirts, ties, and pocket squares). When there was a need to replace worn-out, everyday clothing, and I became aware of how to shop for him, I'd bring home clothing for him to try. Most times, I was pretty on target. I was gratified that he liked what I brought home and it fit; it was a win-win situation all the way around. I look into his closet now and remember where I bought various items and where he wore them. There is warmth in those memories. I couldn't quite articulate early on why I was so connected to his clothes—now, I have words for it. Kate suggested that unless I had a good reason, or felt emotionally ready, I shouldn't be in a hurry or feel pressured to give away Jeff's possessions. I think she's spot on.

Adventure on Joyland Road

***

My memories walk with me and exist in "the stuff" that remains. There are no rules for dealing with loss, nor a playbook on how to handle all the ways our loved ones stay present. For someone like me, my playbook previously consisted of "coloring within the lines," conforming to some definition of socially acceptable, while rigorously analyzing every conceivable option to take in a situation. Now, that seems like a less viable plan. I must try to trust my gut, believing I will know when to stay the course or do something different. I must give as much credence to how I feel about taking a certain path as I do to my logical thought process. I'm open to a different way of coping.

Section 4:
Love and Grief

As is often said, if you've loved someone deeply, then the grief experienced when they pass will be equally profound. There's no way around it—no place to run, and no place to hide. But the love you had, and the space within you where that love existed, remains. It's important to give that love its due and know it's the fuel for your grief. When you reflect on it, would you have preferred never to have loved at all? Not me. Even if it were possible to understand the pain of grief before Jeff died, I wouldn't have changed a moment of our life together. It is a love to be remembered, even as it see-saws with grief. Love and grief walk together, hand-in-hand, just like you did with the one you cherished.

Weaving the Tapestry of Love

Learning and growing to become a better person is a wonderful consequence of being in a loving and reciprocal relationship with a spouse or significant other. In long-term relationships, that process often extends over decades.

Depending on developmental and life circumstances, we occupy different roles with our loved ones. The partnership established isn't solely spousal in nature; it's parental, a friendship, sibling-like, and more—shape-shifting to create a space where two people enrich one another and themselves. When you love someone, you're present in ways that help them grow into their best self. It's an organic process you flow with on a journey we map out with intention, though, in reality, it remains unknowable.

This is why a deep and loving relationship is like weaving a beautiful tapestry. You start with a blank canvas, and with every experience and interaction, a new thread is added, each with a different color and thickness. The layers of time continue this process, which includes the good and the troublesome of what life has to offer. The richness of color and strength of fiber intensify, fleshed out over the crucible of a relationship. And in the end, if the kindness and beauty of love have been yours to share, you have woven a work of art.

My Uncle Simon (Si) had this type of relationship with his wife, Sylvia (Syl). Simon was a remarkable man for his easy-going and positive nature. Sylvia was known as the "little general"—not even 5 feet tall, but formidable in demeanor. Si and Sly had a long, happy marriage of 68 years, producing three sons along the way.

When my uncle was 88 years old, he began to develop some neurological issues related to a fall, including uncontrolled movements of his extremities. Medicine wasn't working to stop these symptoms, so surgery was the next option. The day before Si's surgery I was at the hospital. He was in good spirits, his usual affable self, and communicating clearly. I happened to be in the room with just Syl and him. We talked about how he was feeling and the upcoming surgery, and then the conversation went something like this: He said to Syl, "You know I love you" and she said, "Yes." He told her how beautiful she was, and she laughed and rolled her eyes. Syl was being her usual self—a tough nut to crack. Si was undeterred and pressed on. He said people had asked him if you could love someone for as long as they had been married, and he answered, "*Absolutely yes*," and that he loved her now more than ever.

Si openly and passionately expressed to his wife how much she meant to him and how great his love was for her. Syl smiled and her demeanor softened. I was so riveted by what my uncle was saying to her that I couldn't tear myself away, even though it was such a personal moment between them. It was his love letter to her, and he was emphatic in wanting her to know.

After this five to 10-minute intimate exchange, I went into the hospital hallway to tell my cousins about the amazing conversation I just heard between their parents. I was so grateful to have been present to bear witness and share the story. Si spent the rest of the day and evening alert and kibitzing with his family. He went into surgery the next day, and when he came out, he was in a coma and never regained consciousness. Si passed away a month later. The words he uttered to his wife and family the day before his surgery were the last he ever spoke. Sometimes those who don't have much time left provide great gifts to the rest of us. Si placed the final stroke on his masterpiece.

One brilliant thread of my relationship with Jeff is the story below.

Up, Up, and Away

Jeff and I took a hot-air balloon ride in Colorado several years back. We thought this would be a fun, out-of-the-ordinary vacation activity with minimal risk—even though it involved letting a total stranger take you and another six or seven strangers several hundred feet in the air, without any means to save yourself should something untoward occur.

It was a warm, sunny, cloudless day, and our "captain" seemed confident and in control. As you ascend, the burner heating the air to inflate the balloon is quite noisy. Once you're aloft and being carried by the wind, the burner can be temporarily turned off. You are floating high above the earth in absolute quiet. It's amazing.

It was a beautiful ride; one could view the scenery in every direction—the desert below, rolling hills in the distance, and mountain vistas further on the horizon. Jeff and I, along with our balloon mates, were thoroughly enjoying the experience. But what goes up must eventually come down, and that was when things began to go awry. Unfamiliar at the time with how balloon rides work, an on-the-ground chase team follows the balloon's descent. When the balloon approaches Earth, the chase team stabilizes the basket you are standing in so it doesn't tip over. Once the balloon lands, the burner inflating the balloon must be turned off relatively quickly to reduce the risk of the passengers being turned into human french fries. And once you do that, there's nothing to keep the basket upright. This brings me to the second important function of the chase team—they help you get out of the basket as the sides are relatively high.

After a beautiful and uneventful ride, we discovered the wind currents had taken us off course from our designated landing area.

Adventure on Joyland Road

The chase team was a half hour away and wouldn't reach us for our touchdown to earth. We would have to land without them.

The balloon slowly descended, but as we hovered a few feet above the desert floor, it felt like we were still moving quickly. It wasn't what I or anyone else was expecting—no soft alighting onto a pillow of sand. This is where the chase team is especially handy; they help guide the balloon down and keep you from skidding along the ground into all sorts of desert scrub. Our captain said to hold on and brace ourselves, as we'd be encountering turbulence on the landing. As you might know, hot air balloons aren't equipped with seat belts or body harnesses; they are permanently open-air vehicles. This is not a 747 jet.

We skidded along the ground hitting various scrub vegetation but managed to stay upright. We were all relieved once the balloon came to a complete stop, but the adventure wasn't over yet. The chase team was still 20 minutes away. The balloon needed to be deflated so we didn't risk going up in flames, especially after having just survived the unaided landing. The captain said once the balloon deflated, the basket was definitely going to tip over with all of us in it.

Okay, we were on the ground—the balloon wasn't 100 feet in the air where a tipping accident would've been catastrophic. What's the big deal? The answer to that question depends on which way the balloon tips with eight people inside.

And once the gas was shut off and the balloon began to deflate, it did start to tip—in my direction. Seven other people were beginning to lose their balance, and they were headed in my direction. That's when Jeff sprang, or should I say tilted, into action. He grabbed hold of each side of the basket in spread-eagle fashion where I was cornered, and braced himself for people to fall against him and not directly on me.

I'm often described as "petite" in physical stature. Jeff wasn't a tall man, but he had some girth. He certainly wasn't the type to start a bar fight, but if forced, he wouldn't back down from one either. Jeff valued protecting his family before himself, and in a split second, he spread himself across the basket to keep me from getting hurt.

The basket tipped over, but miraculously, none of us were injured. Because of Jeff, people seemed to shed off on either side of him but not directly on top of me. We all stumbled out, exhilarated to be in one piece and with a new adventure to talk about. The chase team arrived in 10 minutes with the champagne. The practice of concluding a hot-air balloon ride with bubbly refreshment was apparently part of the regional customer experience. In this particular case, it seemed reasonable to have a drink.

Jeff loved this story. He got to be my real-life hero. The handsome prince saving the damsel in distress is a time-honored fairy tale. Jeff was of the era when that romantic and chivalrous story had resonance. Maybe it still does. All I know is that he was my lionheart every day, living a life true to his values.

The Space Where Love Existed

Jeff and I had a big love. Part of my grief exists in that space. Every day I was grateful for Jeff's love and his belief that I was worthy of it. I dearly miss giving my love to someone who so richly deserved it. But it's more than giving my love to this specific person. I learned I have enough space within me to give my love to another human being deeply and live in a reciprocal relationship. There's an emptiness in that shared place, a missing intimacy.

Someone asked me a few months after Jeff died if I would ever marry again. I was a bit stunned by the question. The thought hadn't remotely crossed my mind, and I have no idea if I will ever romantically connect with someone in the future. That same person asked if I was lonely. As I know from my professional work, people ask questions that reveal their anxieties. Death, particularly a sudden death, brings forth all sorts of apprehensions and fears about what life without a partner might look and feel like. I responded to the first question, "No, I hadn't thought about it," and the second question, "No, I'm not lonely, just alone."

The space where our big love once existed now exists without Jeff. But I know the capacity for generous love lives within me. I feel good about that. I don't know whether it will happen again, but I'm not anxious about it. I'm glad I got to share it with him.

Some widows and widowers may have a more urgent desire to fill the internal and external space once occupied by their partner. The aloneness, the quiet, moving through each day and night without the reciprocity of an intimate relationship, is worn differently by surviving spouses. About 10 months after Jeff died, I called a colleague to see how she was doing; her husband had died suddenly a few months before. She told me she had started dating about three to four months after her husband passed away. I wasn't expecting that response. I understand everyone has a different experience with grief and how they cope and move forward. I just couldn't imagine it for myself right then, even though Jeff died six months before my colleague's husband. After the call, I texted my friend, Kate, to tell her about my colleague. Sixty seconds later, the phone rang. It was Kate. She had the same reaction as me.

Kate and I dove into whether there was something wrong with us. We've shared conversations like this since Jeff died and are bound together by our connected experience of loss. We spent the next 10 to 15 minutes trying to figure out why our state of mind differed so vastly from my colleague's. Kate finally said she felt comfortable with her lack of interest in dating because she was still in love with her husband.

That statement hit me like a lightning bolt. It explained so much about how I'd been grieving over the past several months. The love I feel for Jeff is not in the past tense—I am still *in love*, present tense, with my husband. Rather than being weighed down by this thought, I found it freeing. It gave tangible expression and understanding to something I felt but couldn't articulate.

I've been intimately connected with a partner for almost all of my adult life. Actively seeking a partner or companion would appear to be a natural response for me, but it has no appeal right now. Over time, my desire for a deeper interpersonal connection may change; I'm open to where life takes me. For now, I feel a sense of relief and mental clarity that I can acknowledge and express my current state of mind. Thanks, Kate.

Groundhog Day

I was aware that birthdays, anniversaries, and holidays could be tough days to get through emotionally after Jeff died. He passed away in May and his birthday is in November. I tried to prepare myself. A friend asked how I was going to commemorate his birthday. I was glad she asked, and I had thought about it already. I realized I had two choices: do nothing and try not to think about it—which I quickly recognized would leave me feeling bad and guilty all day—or do something to celebrate his memory. I chose the latter.

I had always brought home flowers on Jeff's birthday and did that day, too. He was one of those people for whom it was hard to buy a gift; if he wanted something, he just bought it. Jeff had a very close relationship with Amazon. As you get older, you tend to want fewer things, not more, so consumables like flowers or favorite meals move up the list for birthday celebrations. I placed the flowers in the middle of the kitchen island. I also lit a Yahrzeit candle, a Jewish memorial candle usually lit on the anniversary of a loved one's death, and placed his photo with the flowers and candle. A mini-shrine, I suppose, but it comforted me as I passed by it throughout the day in my kitchen.

The first New Year without him was a tough holiday, and I didn't expect it. Jeff and I never made a big deal out of celebrating the new year. Overpriced restaurant meals, a large proportion of the population driving more poorly than usual, and never being able to stay awake until midnight, made it easy to stay in and cook a nice meal. Yet, when I woke up on New Year's Day, I felt ambushed, my emotions hijacked to a desolate place I had visited before. It was as if I had awakened and found myself on the moon—rocky and barren—with no air to breathe.

I stumbled through the morning, getting teary and unable to pinpoint exactly why. And then it hit me—I was facing an entire new year of waking up every morning without Jeff—my own personal Groundhog Day. If you aren't familiar with the Bill Murray movie, Groundhog Day, here's a brief synopsis. Murray is a TV newsman on assignment with his crew covering Groundhog Day in Punxsutawney, Pennsylvania. He wakes up every morning to relive the same day over and over, until he changes into a nicer human and falls in love with his leading lady, Andie MacDowell. Movies involve a suspension of disbelief, which is how we immerse ourselves in them. But the suspension of disbelief is not how death works. It's unfortunately real and must be dealt with in some fashion by the living.

At the moment I'm writing this, I've yet to come to the anniversary of Jeff's passing. I anticipate the force of that day will be exponentially greater than New Year's, but the issue will be the same: it will highlight my very real Groundhog Day. I'll try to make a plan to avoid spiraling into an emotional nosedive, but I can't say it's not going to happen.

Like the movie, I wake up every morning to the same reality—Jeff isn't there. What I do with the rest of the day is up to me.

***

It's now about a year and a half since Jeff died, and I am turning 70 years old. My friend, Kate, threw herself a 70th birthday luncheon for her close women friends earlier in the year. In the midst of getting the home she shared with her husband for decades ready for sale, continuing to work, and engaging in her professional organization commitments, Kate threw herself a birthday luncheon. I understand why. Kate is a vibrant, healthy 70-year-old. She's moving into this chronological milestone as a widow, without the dream of living out the rest of her life with the person she loved the most. Despite all the other life responsibilities weighing on her, how she would negotiate—let alone celebrate—becoming 70 years old without her husband seemed most pressing. Boy, do I get it.

Kate reminded me that her husband was also her best friend. The idea that your husband is your best friend is a concept I never questioned. As the fairy tale goes, you find a partner you romantically love and with whom you share a true friendship. You never run out of things to talk and laugh about, and there's never enough time to spend together. Jeff was certainly my best friend, and that's how it's supposed to be, right? Perhaps so, but the story in real life doesn't always work out that way.

I suppose I was a bit naïve about the implications of being such a romantic, but it explains why some things are so hard to do now. Kate and I consider ourselves independent, competent women who can take care of ourselves. Our self-esteem didn't suffer from the death of our husbands; we can move through the world in a way that looks no different than it did when our spouses were alive. And, yet, I'm reluctant to do certain things Jeff and I did before, like go on a vacation. I used to do those things with my best friend, my husband. Will I eventually find friends to travel with? Sure. But a sense of melancholy comes over me when I think about it, draining my motivation to act. My best and most intimate friend is no longer here to share those moments with me.

Both Kate's husband and Jeff—had they still been present on this earth for our milestone 70th birthdays—would've taken us out for a memorable meal and a celebratory cocktail. They would have told us how fabulous we looked and that 70 is the new 50. Kate and I would've raised an eyebrow and replied with a smirky, "Sure," but been secretly delighted they said it. Like the fine wine we might have been drinking that night, we would've most enjoyed the subtlety and smoothness of our respective relationships—talking, laughing, and creating one more precious moment.

But our husbands aren't here to share this significant time in our lives, so celebrating with and gathering strength from a posse of friends seemed the way to go. As I'm lucky enough to be Kate's friend, I got to experience how this idea worked firsthand. Kate's friends are as devoted to her as she is to them. Kate had all the regular birthday trappings at her party—decorations, lunch, cake, and lots of talk and laughter. She gave a birthday speech before she cut the cake, telling us how important we were in her life. Kate talked about her late husband and his unseen presence at the party. How could he *not* be there in spirit on this momentous occasion?

Although I've done a lot of public speaking in my life and am comfortable being the center of attention, my birthday is not one of those times where I wish to be in the spotlight. I like to educate and entertain as I think I have something to offer. Celebrating the circumstance of having lived another year seems an unnecessary focus for having done nothing out of the ordinary. Yet, none of Kate's birthday celebration was lost on me.

What I learned from Kate was not to ignore this moment in time. I thought it would be Jeff's birthday or our anniversary that would bother me most when those events inevitably rolled around. But I was troubled, in an unexpected way, that Jeff wasn't here to celebrate this "big" birthday with me. I needed to find a way not just to manage my grief over one more memory Jeff and I would never create, but also to celebrate having made it to my seventh decade. I consciously decided to acknowledge and enjoy this milestone birthday and share it with the people I cared about most.

So, I decided to throw myself a birthday party too. As the date of my birthday approached, I thought I better start making plans. But throwing yourself a party is a lot of work, and I procrastinated. I knew I'd more than regret doing nothing, but I was ambivalent about the effort required to plan and implement a party—as noted by my lack of action. And, then, like a shot in the dark, the answer to how I would celebrate my 70th birthday appeared. My good friend, Mason, told me he and his spouse would like to take me to a nice restaurant *on my birthday*. Bingo! I love Mason and his husband and couldn't think of two better people to be with that day.

    Soon after, the ladies in my building said they wanted to take me to lunch for my birthday. These remarkable women, my dear friends, treated me to lunch at a charming local restaurant. Amazing! After that, I decided my strategy would be to have as many mini-celebrations as I could with the people I care about. I asked my cousins to come to my house for dinner. Kate and I took ourselves to dinner at a nice restaurant to celebrate both of our birthdays. We talked about our husbands as much as we wanted, and no one lifted an eyebrow. It all felt right to me.

    It's worth repeating—every day I wake up and know Jeff won't be there. How I spend the rest of the day is up to me.

My Lodestar

Jeff was nine years my senior. He was 47 and I was 38 when we married. Our first date was about 15 months earlier. He was kind, smart, and funny, checking off all the criteria that are really important in a relationship. But he was way more than that. Jeff was a person of great moral character—thoroughly honest, emotionally patient, and generous. At the age of 38, I still had a lot more growing up to do. Perhaps a more accurate phrase is "growing better."

I used to joke that being married to a psychiatrist—specifically Jeff—the 24/7 therapy was doing wonders for me, but I was only half kidding. I was headstrong and stubborn, thinking I knew the best way, not finding it easy to see that wasn't always true. But I met my match with Jeff, and over time, through great patience on his part, I managed to glimpse my flaws. Being a perfectionist is a grueling business. Giving yourself a break and learning from your mistakes is a much better path to follow.

You might think I've glorified my husband to the point of lacking any objectivity. Was Jeff perfect, no. Sometimes I thought I was living with a 14-year-old. He was not one to put his clothes away at the end of the day, not in 30 years. In the morning, I'd find his jeans half-standing on the floor in the same position he'd walked out of them the night before. Nor was he inclined to cook, not that I would let him after he whiffed on what it meant to marinate, not drown, two fish filets. These were small inconveniences I wisely chose not to care about. They didn't matter in the grand scheme of things.

Jeff didn't whiff on being a loving and supportive husband and father. He was my greatest cheerleader and my best critic. He would tell me I was beautiful even as I aged and saw my looks fade into sun spots and wrinkles. Vanity is a cruel thing, yet every time Jeff told me I was beautiful, I always felt a little better. What mattered was that *he* still found me beautiful and cared enough to say so.

Physical beauty, as defined by Western culture, is a very poor criterion to use for measuring the value of another human being. I almost made that mistake before I even met Jeff.

When Jeff and I first talked in 1992, there was no Facetime. I heard his deep voice on the other end of the phone, but there was no social media to check out what he might look like. My clumsy attempt to have Jeff reveal his appearance led him to honestly answer he was "bald and middle-aged." I was thinking Sigmund Freud-ish, which was okay by me. I was never one to count a straight nose or a full head of hair as high on my list of important features for judging the measure of another human.

A few days after Jeff and I arranged our first date, I saw my colleague, Linda, who had fixed us up. I told her Jeff called, he sounded intriguing, and we set a day and time to meet. She then said, "You know, he's fat." "What?" I exclaimed. I believe Linda thought Jeff and I would be a good match in many ways but chose this moment to be completely forthcoming. I was rattled. I've been slim my whole life, probably a combination of genetics and how I care for my body. I indicated I wasn't interested in dating someone who was obese. She quickly responded, "He was really overweight, but he lost 80 pounds." I started to breathe again and said to myself, "Okay, try not to jump to conclusions. This is someone trying to take care of himself." I'm not proud of my immediate response as I reflect on it today; it was shallow and biased. One can only hope to learn that quickly drawn assumptions about the merits of another human being can be dead wrong.

As I approached the restaurant for our first date, I saw Jeff stepping out of his car. That thought about him being obese, thankfully, didn't enter my head. And, of course, as I got to know Jeff, all the other amazing characteristics he possessed—his generosity, integrity, intelligence, and humor—were on display. Over the course of our marriage, Jeff did get heavier. He struggled with his weight for many years; it was a lifelong issue. But I cared about his weight in relation to his health, not how he looked. I didn't see fat. I saw someone I deeply loved and who I wanted to outlive me.

And I saw Jeff as physically beautiful, even when he was overweight. Jeff never spent time in the sun, as his fair skin would begin to turn red before he could get comfortable in a lounge chair. Baseball caps were an absolute packing essential should we be headed to sunnier skies. Even as he aged, his skin never got dry or scaly. I'd tell Jeff his skin "felt like velvet," and it did. Though he was bald, the hair he did have was soft and downy. And I unequivocally loved his beard: it was thick and smooth, a truly killer beard. I never let him shave it off. Jeff liked fine clothing for fancier occasions—beautiful ties and well-made suits. When we would get dressed up for a wedding, I'd tell him he looked gorgeous. He'd answer, "No, you're gorgeous" and then we would go back and forth, teasingly complimenting each other. But I meant it, he was beautiful in my eyes.

I wasn't a bad person before I knew Jeff, but knowing him and watching how he moved through the world made me a better one. I want to keep evolving into some enhanced form of myself, not perfect but kinder, gentler, and more patient. That would be quite the legacy.

Woodstock

One of Jeff's favorite stories was that he attended the Woodstock musical festival in 1969. But it wasn't in the way you might think.

For those of the Baby Boomer Generation, the Woodstock Music and Art Festival was historic and iconic in the annals of musical festivals. Woodstock was celebrated as a festival of "peace, love, and music." It represented a counter-culture of young people who peacefully gathered under, what turned out to be, challenging circumstances to listen to great music and enjoy each other's company, in both natural and mind-altering states. And the musicians who performed—Richie Havens, Joan Baez, Ravi Shankar, the Grateful Dead, Jefferson Airplane, Crosby, Stills & Nash, Jimi Hendrix, Santana, the Band, and many more—were spectacular. The festival was originally conceived as a for-profit venture ($18 in advance for the three-day event, $24 at the gate), but quickly turned into a free concert when young people from all over the country descended upon upstate New York and overwhelmed the area where the festival was held. Woodstock was an unforeseen, organic moment in time that was astonishing in the way it played out and the legacy it left.

Jeff was a fourth-year medical student and home for the summer. Monticello, NY is about 30 minutes from Bethel, NY, and Max Yasgur's dairy farm, where the festival was happening. Like many small towns around the festival, Monticello pitched in to help feed the throngs of young people who showed up to attend. Roads were blocked for miles with cars that had nowhere to go. The only way into the festival after the first day was by foot or air.

The National Guard was also trying to assist, flying a helicopter in and out of Woodstock for medical emergencies. On Saturday morning of the festival, a local state legislator decided he wanted to take a birds-eye view of the proceedings. Jeff, and his friend, Sam, were at the local high school to help prepare food and where arrangements were being made to fly the legislator in. A National Guard officer asked if anyone could help on-site in the medical tent. Having almost finished medical school, Jeff said he could lend a hand. And, after all, attending Woodstock was a ready-made, once-in-a-lifetime adventure.

They included Jeff as a passenger in the helicopter, albeit with his legs hanging out over the open side. As the chopper lifted off, Jeff yelled to Sam on the ground, "Tell my mother." Jeff was pretty sure Sam was in a much more precarious position.

When the helicopter approached a grassy, verdant crest of the Yasgur farm, the scenery abruptly changed to a sea of beige on the other side of the hill—humans, in massive numbers. It's estimated that almost half a million people attended Woodstock throughout the four-day event.

The helicopter landed close to the medical tent located behind the stage. It was an incredible scene with the sheer mass of humanity and controlled chaos. Jeff was mighty interested in checking things out where the music was playing, but he responsibly went into the medical tent. The physician in charge asked what duties he was capable of performing. At Woodstock many attendees chose to go barefoot, so foot lacerations were the most common injury. Jeff said he could do suturing. At that time, Jeff was considering two options for his residency—psychiatry or surgery—after he graduated from medical school. Those two choices seem like polar opposites, but Jeff had great dexterity with his hands and using tools, so being a surgeon seemed like a specialty to consider. I and a lot of other people are grateful he chose psychiatry.

But by the time Jeff arrived that Saturday morning, the medical staff had already run out of sterile suture kits and were stitching people up with Coats and Clark—as in the sewing thread. The risk of infection rises substantially without sterile sutures, but then there's the immediate issue of closing gaping wounds. Jeff said he could also triage patients (deciding who has a more critical illness or wound and should be treated sooner), so the staff had him go with that. Jeff was able to identify a young woman with suspected acute appendicitis who was flown out later that day. If you haven't seen *Woodstock: Three Days that Defined a Generation*, it's a terrific documentary about the event; it includes some music but focuses more on what happened behind the scenes. And I could swear I glimpsed the back of Jeff, just for a brief moment, helping to carry a stretcher into the medical tent.

By late in the day, a last flight was going out for the evening. Jeff thought it might be best to leave then, not knowing what the reception would be from his mother when he returned home. As twilight approached, he boarded the helicopter, flew back to the school, and walked home. Upon entering his house his mother was waiting. Her first stern words were, "Go take a shower!"

Jeff loved this story. He must have told it a hundred times during our marriage. I never stopped him, even though I'd heard it countless times before. I knew he loved telling the story for its unusual twist, and though he saw none of the musical acts, he attended in a most unique way.

After Jeff died, I didn't hear that story for many months—until I told it. An appropriate context arose to share his Woodstock story with some friends who'd never heard it. I recounted it with all the relish and enthusiasm that he did. I felt so alive with his memory when I was telling the story. It was a gratifying moment I didn't expect, like he was right there with me.

Lisa Rosenberg

Jeff had a few stories from his life he liked to tell people. I heard them many times over the years, and now, I'm so glad I did. They burn bright in my memory—an oral history of him that lives on through me.

The Unseen Presence

It's been about 10 months since Jeff has passed. My heart is still heavy with his loss. I carry him with me—sometimes like a sentient being, other times like a shadow. He's always there, nonetheless. C.S. Lewis deeply suffered the loss of his wife. In *A Grief Observed* he speaks to the breadth of his anguish, "Her absence is like the sky, spread over everything." People who have lost an intimate loved one know this feeling. You go about your day and interact with others without their sensing this part of your internal life. And after a year goes by, then another, and another, I don't know if this continual counterplay between living life and experiencing your loved one's unseen presence—or absence—ever diminishes or resolves.

Perhaps what's so clear to me now is that one of the things I miss the most is simply hanging out with Jeff. There's a sense of ease in being with someone you're completely comfortable with, whose belches and farts carry no objectionable meaning. On the contrary, they're a reminder that your loved one is alive and present, living their life right in front of you, even if you wrinkle your nose or make a mocking comment. That person is someone with whom you can be vulnerable like no other; where sitting, reading, or watching TV together is what you'd rather be doing than almost anything else. The big celebrations or events in life—wedding anniversaries, a job promotion, an amazing vacation—are all wonderful to share and remember, but "the hanging out" is what presses into me most and what I pine for.

There are also more ephemeral moments that cross my mind, where the experience of great intimacy brought on a state of being in which time and space lost their form and relevance, and Jeff and I were bound together in a cocoon of affection and tenderness. Those unique and precious moments of feeling connected to another human being, along with the quietly remarkable years of simply being with each other, make Jeff indelible in my mind. He is a presence I can never unsee or unsense.

The feeling of absence, a corollary to your loved one's unseen presence, has a form and texture all its own; you can almost touch it, but not quite, and it shape-shifts. Sometimes, it's a sharp stick that unexpectedly pokes you in the ribs. Other times, this sense of your loved one's absence feels more amorphous, surrounding you in an infinite space of dotted lines. Just when you slip through, seemingly free to go as you please, you cross back into a place of fully knowing you'll never experience their earthly presence again. It is a journey of bobbing and weaving with life as it now exists, jabbing and counterpunching with the invisible phantom of absence. Perhaps absence and I will call a truce one day and find a way to co-exist more peacefully. I'm just not sure yet.

I wonder if others, who have yet to experience the pain that is the flip side of passion, have a sense of this aspect of the grieving process. We don't talk about grief well or comfortably in Western society. After a year of grieving, I would guess most people think you've had enough time to "get over it," and you shouldn't be thinking about the loss of your loved one so much. I'm not talking about ruminating over the loss to the point of functional impairment. I'm referring to the way the soul of your loved one is embedded in you. It cannot be excised or surgically removed. It becomes an ethereal part of you that can't be seen or heard by others, but you know is always present.

Perhaps that is the problem. It's hard to talk about something others cannot sense. If you did, you risk them thinking you're living in the past, wallowing in self-pity, and not getting on with your life. On the other hand, giving voice to this internal life may allow for living more fully in the present. It seems that first I need to accept the existence of a new internal frame of reference—me and the other, who can no longer be seen.

In acknowledging that I carry Jeff with me, not as a burden but as a flickering light that dances across my consciousness, I've become less concerned about what others think of me. When I'm with people, and an appropriate context arises for me to tell a "Jeff story," I do. I've told his Woodstock story and the saga of his parents coming to America a few times. I always feel good about sharing his life stories, allowing his presence to be seen by others and perhaps even benefit from it. Some people will understand why his presence remains close at hand for me, others may not. I'll have to be okay with that.

May 20

May 20th is the anniversary of Jeff's death. On June 16, 2023, we had the dedication or unveiling of Jeff's headstone. In Jewish tradition, the ceremony is usually conducted within the first year after the person has passed away, but there's no firm timeline. The custom of placing a headstone or monument over the grave of a loved one goes back to ancient biblical times. It's noted in the Book of Genesis that Jacob, to honor his wife, Rachel, placed a tombstone at the head of her grave. In more modern times, a ceremony is conducted to "unveil" the headstone where prayers are said, family share thoughts of their loved one, and a white cloth is removed to reveal the monument. It's meant to be a time when friends and family comfort each other and remember the person who passed away.

These are the words I spoke at Jeff's dedication:

I will:

Sense your presence as my life unfolds without you
Smile when recalling how you always made me laugh
Share our memories with anyone who will listen
Know your warm embrace in the caressing summer breeze
Hear your wise counsel as challenges inevitably arise
Feel your "angel kisses" brushing my forehead
Speak of you with love and kindness until I have no voice

Adventure on Joyland Road

Remember everything about you.

I will walk this earth until I no longer can and then fly away with you into the mist.

—

I made a very measured decision in burying my husband, your father, your grandfather, your cousin, your friend in a national cemetery. Jeff was my rock, my hero, my best critic, and greatest cheerleader, and I didn't want him to ever be forgotten. This is a place where he will never be forgotten.

I want to thank all of you for the love and support you have shown me over the last year. It has been a life raft for me in a sea of unexpected grief. I am so very grateful to have you in my life.

During the dedication of Jeff's headstone, all the grandchildren placed stones on its curved top until there was no room for another. Within the Jewish faith, it's customary to leave a small stone on the monument when visiting a gravesite to signify someone has come to honor the deceased. It's a tangible way of commemorating the burial and the person who passed away. Stones, sturdy and ever-present since the dawn of time, serve as a fitting reminder of the enduring presence of the departed's life and memory.

I surely thought all those little rocks, precariously placed by small hands, would be driven to the ground after a good wind or rain storm. But, somehow, that did not occur. Through heavy gusts of wind and driving rain, they have, by and large, managed to stay perched on top of the headstone. Yes, I've picked up one or two of the smaller ones and placed them back in their rightful positions, but this symphony of stones has managed to stubbornly stay put. And the cemetery landscape crew has been ever respectful in leaving them undisturbed. I find it a bit miraculous, and as I approach Jeff's gravesite, trying to spy these little stone soldiers from afar, I'm comforted by their staying power.

These wondrous pieces of earth are like miniature Rocks of Gibraltar, symbolizing the enduring love that remains.

Caressed by warm breezes or cut by harsh winds
Stroked by a gentle rain or pelted by a torrential downpour
Warmed on a sunny day or chilled by the clouds overhead,
the stones persist,
Signifying a sea of memories for those who choose not to forget.

***

To this day, I visit Fort Sheridan National Cemetery about once a week. That may seem excessive to some, but it isn't for me. I can walk to Jeff's gravesite from my home; it's adjacent to the nature paths and part of the historic area where I live. People come from all over the Chicago metro area to walk the trails and view scenic vistas overlooking Lake Michigan, which flank the cemetery.

Fort Sheridan National Cemetery holds significant historical context. It was established in 1889, with the first burials dating back to Civil War veterans. Men who fought with the 7th Cavalry under General George Custer are buried there. All but one were survivors of the Battle of Little Bighorn, fought in June 1876. Because Fort Sheridan served as the Midwest administrative center for WWII prisoner-of-war camps, nine German prisoners of war who died during their confinement were buried in the cemetery. There's also a memorial to young Ervin Staples, a Private 1st Class who died during the Battle of the Bulge in December 1944. His body was never recovered.

The grounds of the cemetery, though mostly symmetrical, aren't completely so. The landscape construction is oval, with an outer ring of graves divided into 12 sections of varying size. "It is a place of peaceful reflection" as noted in the information posted at the cemetery entrance. Most of the headstones are uniform, rectangular with a curved, sloping top, but not all. Early gravesites were allowed unique headstones, but that practice stopped decades ago—along with casket burials—in favor of cremation and the uniform headstone style now common in places like Arlington National Cemetery. A large circular area in the center of the cemetery had been an open expanse of grass since its founding. That was, until recently.

I buried Jeff's ashes in December 2022, when fewer than 30 gravesites were available in the outer ring of the cemetery. By early spring, all of those sites were occupied, and the center ring opened for new gravesites. The Baby Boomer generation and the Vietnam era coincided to create a need for more veteran burials. Over the years, the sections have become denser and veterans are buried more closely together. In the center section, an area that doesn't seem so large, the plan is to inter another 2600 veterans. In a plot of land recently purchased by the U.S. government, just behind the existing cemetery, a columbarium is planned for another 10,000 veterans.

Fort Sheridan Cemetery is beautifully cared for and surrounded by tall trees and open land. It is serene, a place you can visit and talk to the one you love. Other people who don't know your loved one visit, too, out of respect for those buried there and to remember their sacrifice. When I take a long walk with my neighbors and the trail inevitably takes us by the cemetery, I ask if we might stop to visit Jeff's grave. My friends are gracious and don't mind stopping by to say hello, they knew him, too. Mostly, though, they are being kind to me, understanding my need to take a few extra steps so I can be close to Jeff's memory.

The cemetery is the embodiment of stability and change intermixed over the decades. Even the military couldn't avoid the inevitable changes that time compels to accommodate the burial of more people who served our country. That is a metaphor not lost on me. Just when we think we have the right life strategy, the profession we trained for, and the love of our lives, something happens. Suddenly, things are different and our perspective changes—the job isn't fulfilling, there's a divorce, someone dies—we are forced to adapt. The landscape has shifted beneath our feet and we're scrambling to regain our balance, trying to find a way to right ourselves and keep moving forward.

Section 5:
Sometimes There Are No Answers

As much as we seek comfort, answers, relief—a balm for our aching hearts—sometimes there aren't any answers. We often succeed in finding some tranquility and allowing ourselves blessed rest from the constancy of our loss, but not always. We must come to some détente with the notion that every once in a while, a feeling, a thought, or a question will arise that is unsolvable and immutable. It's best to acknowledge its presence and find a peaceful way to live with it.

Tears Without Warning

I wasn't much of a crier before Jeff died. Particularly in my younger days, long periods would go by without me shedding a tear. I was stiff-upper-lipped at sad events and didn't blubber at the happy endings of romantic comedies. There is one surprising exception to my no-crying declaration. I cried each time a grandchild was born, overcome by the joy of their arrival and the possibilities ahead. But mostly, I was not a crier.

It's worth a moment to reflect on why I might've been this way. I value being practical and solution-oriented; thus, it seems essential to maintain control of my internal and external environments—if you get emotional, you can't think straight. Also, my self-imposed persona, for better or worse, is that I'm a tough guy. Being a tough guy extends into both the emotional and physical realms. Jeff was concerned I might get into big trouble one day with that whole tough guy routine, and because size does matter in some situations, he tried to convince me I was more like a cornered Chihuahua.

Jeff was not a big crier either. He adhered to the male persona of being strong and stalwart when facing emotional and physical discomfort. I watched him withstand great physical pain any number of times—falls, surgeries, wound debridement. Most people, including me, would've been moaning or screaming at what I saw him endure. In every circumstance, he remained calm and didn't flinch or cry out; he just sat there and took it. I guess watching his dad, and all of those old cowboy and war movies of his youth, made an impression on him and internalized a "manly" behavior to emulate.

But Jeff's eyes would well up and his voice would change tenor for one circumstance in particular—sweet romantic comedies. Seriously, yes, romantic movies got to him. He loved the movie, Serendipity. The star, John Cusack, spends the entire film looking all over New York City for a woman he met by chance; he believes she's the love of his life. The movie is funny, charming, and romantic. I think Jeff believed in that type of romance—where fairy tales really can come true. Maybe he thought it happened to him. I know it did for me. Every time Jeff watched Serendipity, I teased him at the end because his eyes would betray his emotions. He would tease back and ask what was the matter with me for not getting choked up. In our last years together, I did begin to get more emotional about sad and romantic things, but I chalked that up to getting older and becoming more sentimental.

Now, since Jeff's death, behind every poignant thought is a vale of tears. My eyes well up at a mere idea or a song that reminds me of him or a tender memory that breaks my heart for a fleeting moment. I can't control the fountain of sentiment that quickly surges forth and spills out of me.

In the months shortly after Jeff's death, if a teary episode happened at the end of the day, I was often exhausted by the emotion of it. I would go to sleep and hope the following morning I found myself in a more peaceful condition; perhaps I'd stumble upon some new insight from being in a dream-like state. Upon awakening, if no insights had revealed themselves, I pushed myself into the day's activities. I called a friend or family member or checked in with a neighbor, trying to find some way to get myself grounded. Other times, identifying the temporal event—like an upcoming birthday or anniversary— that had attached itself to a sudden fit of sobbing provided some mental relief. If you can ascertain the cause of the distress, it will allow you to process the emotion, so my logical reasoning goes. Logic doesn't always work, though.

Over a year and a half after Jeff died, I was caught in one of those sudden eruptions of tears. I found this could happen when doing some mundane task, like watering the plants or putting groceries away—a thought breaks through and stops me in my tracks. It was a brutally cold January day, -8 degrees in real temperature and a wind chill of -25 to -30. The ice framed the inside of each window in my apartment, stubbornly refusing to evaporate; it was just too cold outside. I'd been to the grocery store and could feel how bone-chilling and dangerous the weather was. When I returned to my snug, warm home, a horrifying thought exploded into my consciousness—that my Jeff was out there on his own, buried in the cold, frozen ground. He was alone, and I couldn't help him.

Weeping, I went to his photograph in the hallway and stood before it. As irrational as it may seem, I apologized, saying over and over I was so sorry I wasn't there to take care of him, be with him, and make sure he was okay. Perhaps, religion would've been of great benefit here. At times, I try to believe there is some higher power and because Jeff was a good and deserving person, he will forever walk in Elysian Fields. But that is not this moment, so I cry until the weeping subsides and I slowly re-engage with the world. It's like being caught in a cold, drenching rain. Damp and shivering, I search for shelter and wait for the storm to pass. Those tears carry a vital essence of me that now must be replenished. How do you put rain back in the sky?

I attended an event at my former university several months after Jeff died. A number of my faculty colleagues were also in attendance. I like these people, and had worked with them for decades, so I visited several tables to say hello. One of the women, Chris, who I hadn't seen since I retired, lost her husband suddenly when she was in her mid-30s, leaving her heartbroken and with two young children to raise. She's an amazing person for her grit and fortitude. After several

Adventure on Joyland Road

years, Chris remarried. We greeted each other warmly and chatted about her job and now college-age children. Chris then disclosed she'd been thinking about me. It was over 20 years since her first husband had died. She became teary and said not a day goes by when she doesn't think about him. Another colleague, whom I also hadn't seen since my retirement, lost her husband a number of years prior. She said virtually the same thing to me; her eyes welled up, and she told me I'd been on her mind. Her face was tight with the memory of loss and how it stays with you, writ large at that moment, because someone stands before you in the same regrettable circumstance.

I've concluded that some days will be sadder and tearier than others. Sometimes those tears are related to existential thoughts that dive deep into perilous waters, wanting to fathom the unknowable. You can get stuck in the depths of what it means to be alone and wonder, "Will it always be that way in this life and the next?" Finding the oxygen to resurface is a challenge.

Whatever brings on the tears, sobbing, and outright weeping, it's okay to let it happen. Shoving the emotion down the stairs to some subterranean basement where I'd like it to live, out of sight and out of mind, doesn't work. It's like the Dutch proverb of putting your finger in the dike to keep it from bursting; it will only hold off the impending deluge for a little while. You just have to go with it and find your way through it.

Going to the Airport Is a Killer

My chest feels like it's filled with lead right now. I should be excited to go out of town, but my heart is slowly sinking into the backseat of the taxi. When Jeff and I would finally get in a cab after the angst of packing was over, plants watered, and the front door locked behind us, my sense of anticipation was palpable. Breaking the routine of our normal professional lives was such a welcome respite. Now, all I can think about is that Jeff isn't here to share the adventure.

I'll drag this sadness with me into O'Hare Airport and through TSA. While I wait to board the plane, I'll silently worry about whether there will be enough space left in the overhead bins for my carry-on bag. When Jeff and I would travel together, and finally settle into our seats, I'd lean over and rest my head against his shoulder. It wasn't something I did elsewhere in public, just on a plane. Jeff was not one for public displays of affection, but on a plane, he was captive! I took advantage of the moment, and he let me. Oh, those sweet, small vignettes of what life used to be.

Now, I need to stay focused without a co-pilot to rely on. I can't let myself sink into the quicksand of all those lost moments. I'll gradually snap out of it when I reach my destination, where family, friends, or colleagues are waiting for me. I hate this feeling of not being fully present. At these moments, I am a shadow.

When I get to my destination and have to engage in the

consultation work I do, I'm completely focused and committed; I am fully myself. I'm surprised I can still be who I was—capable, funny, energetic. But I don't miss Jeff any less. When I return to my hotel room at the end of the day, I want to call and tell him how my day went and ask about his—which friends he touched base with and what he ate for dinner that evening. When I go to sleep, I still tell him I love him. These juxtapositions create a sense of disequilibrium: feeling like the genuine, old me and, moments later, the hollowed-out me. How all this eventually melds together is a work in progress.

On one consulting trip to Washington, D.C., I couldn't arrange dinner with any of my colleagues one evening, so I went to a well-known and crowded restaurant close to my hotel. As a single diner, I chose to eat at the bar. The place was popular with the young D.C. after-work crowd, and incredibly noisy. The service wasn't good and the food was even worse. The longer I stayed, the more desperate I was to leave. As I impatiently waited for my long-lost server to appear with the check, David Brooks, the New York Times columnist and author, passed by where I was seated. As I'm a big fan (or geek), an awful dining experience somehow felt a little less dreadful. I was excited to rush back to my hotel room and call Jeff to tell him I just saw David Brooks. Within a millisecond, I realized that was not going to be possible. Each of those once-cherished moments has become a sharp, quick sting of reality that I now must find a way to move past.

After the return flight to O'Hare in the early evening, the taxi driver delivers me home. The same sinking feeling that flooded me on the way to the airport slowly seeps back into my body—a rising tide of dread I do not wish to examine. I open the front door, and there it is again, fully smacking me in the face: the house is too quiet, too still. I'm confronted with the realization that Jeff isn't here and never will be.

In retrospect, when Jeff was there to greet me, glad to see me but not wishing to appear he was lonely without me, those first moments of walking in the door felt so grounding. I was back in our shared and intimate space, our orbits aligned to circle each other in a dance only we knew. As much as I try to prepare my mind, I don't know if I'll ever get over feeling deflated every time I return home and unlock the door. The embedded nature of two lives entwined can find its voice at unexpected times. But sometimes the voice has no sound and can only be heard in the stillness of the night.

Decisions, Decisions, Decisions

When he was alive, I talked to Jeff—a lot. So much, in fact, that sometimes he would feign relief when I lost my voice after catching a bad cold. He said I was "encyclopedic" when I had to make a decision, needing to consider every possible option before hitting the add-to-cart button. He wasn't wrong as that's exactly what I do. If I'm buying scissors online: Are the blades sharp and made of stainless steel? Is the handle ergonomic? I'm sure I drove Jeff to distraction more than once.

I thought about my penchant for engaging in these mental gymnastics when I was laid low by a stomach virus for a couple of days. I was considering canceling a dinner with friends but felt ambivalent about canceling. Was I being too quick in making that decision? Maybe I'd feel better later in the day. I know it's good for me to be out with people and engaged socially, would I regret my decision later? I had no one to ask, no one to complain to, no one to share my misery with. In short, no Jeff. I went into a tailspin, realizing I no longer had the presence of a loving partner who relieved me of making every last decision and supported me with kind words.

What's so special about sharing with a trusted partner? Every time it happened when Jeff was alive, it was a small unseen miracle of relief. Someone to discuss my worries with, help me weigh the options, and share in making thoughtful decisions. You do it so often with your spouse or significant other over the years that you start to take for granted just how exquisite those interactions truly are.

I tell myself Jeff lives inside me, existing in some internalized form that will help guide me. While there is truth to that, I took little solace when I had to decide whether to cancel a dinner engagement. And the funny thing is, it wasn't a big decision, like should I sell the house or buy a new car. It was a small one, but so many small ones seem more complicated than they should be. And a bigger one, I figure I need a plan and a half to get through it. It's exhausting.

In this new life, I have no wingman to share the responsibility of all the decision-making, big or small, and no amount of wishful thinking will change that. Yes, I can talk to friends and family if I need help making certain decisions, but most of my talking is to myself, reflecting inward about what to do and when to do it. I understood soon after Jeff died that I would need to be fully responsible for owning my life. My structured, exhaustive way of approaching decision-making before Jeff's death serves me reasonably well most of the time, but that's not the issue. The process of sharing and aligning with someone attuned to who you are—all your foibles and fears, and more noble qualities—is what I miss so terribly much.

Expect the Unexpected

If you're of a certain age, you'll know the child's toy, Pop Goes the Weasel or Jack-in-the-Box. It consists of a small metal box with a crank. As you begin to turn the crank, a simple melody plays. When the coil inside is tightly wound, it springs the lid off the top of the box, and a cute animal or clown pops up. This toy is a delight for very young children. The surprise and glee they experience every time something pops out is enchanting.

I'm reminded of the "pop goes the weasel" experience during this period of my life, but not in such a pleasant way. It's been close to a year since Jeff passed away, and I'm still surprised by unexpected events that stun me with their emotional impact.

Jeff and I shared credit cards like probably most couples do. Although we each had a card with our name on it, he was listed as the primary cardholder, even though both our assets were considered when the card was issued. We used a particular card for many years, and the benefits suited our lifestyle. I never gave much thought to the fact that I wasn't the primary cardholder. But the credit card company does care. When I told the company my husband was deceased, they immediately canceled the card, leaving me high and dry. It was like an invisible laser had found my wallet and instantly vaporized that piece of plastic. Sure, they told me, I could re-apply for a card in my name, but no, I couldn't have the old card with the same benefits. It didn't matter if I had paid every previous bill on time and was a loyal, long-term customer—there was no going back, no re-creating what was.

That unexpected event triggered a dizzying array of issues to resolve and solutions to consider. What about all my monthly auto-pay bills on the canceled credit card? How quickly could I get another card? Which company offered benefits similar to the old card? I needed to quickly sort through all of those practical matters.

But I became irritated and agitated by this incident, more so than I would've imagined. I don't lack self-confidence in my ability to tackle issues head-on and problem-solve. Yet, I was angry with the credit card company for their actions, ones I suspect they must immediately enforce to prevent the fraudulent use of a dead man's credit.

After a conversation with myself, I realized what upset me. It was one more thing that represented us—this stupid credit card—being unceremoniously ripped away, and I could do nothing about it. Another piece of our dual, Jeff-and-Lisa identity was being erased, torn from me without my consent. The canceled credit card was the weasel that popped out of the box.

On the practical side, lesson learned, I can tell you it's always a good idea to be the primary holder of a credit card. As to the emotional side, this event was one more aspect of suffering the loss, and I couldn't keep it from happening. As much as I wanted to control my fate and hang onto this piece of our identity, I was ultimately powerless to do so.

Note to self: Over time, I'm sure other unexpected emotional minefields will throw me for a loop, even as they sit plainly in front of me. It's probably prudent to have the mindset that, as the months and years pass, the element of surprise remains in play, hidden in the innocence of everyday, untoward occurrences.

***

And so it goes. A few months after I wrote the above, a small landmine arrived in the mail—a letter addressed to Jeff notifying him

Adventure on Joyland Road

of his driver's license renewal. He was of the age where a vision and road test would need to be taken for his license to be renewed. It was all clearly explained in a letter from the Secretary of the State of Illinois. But Jeff wouldn't be taking a driver's test now or ever, unless they let him cruise in a sapphire-blue Porsche 911 Carrera on some winding, heavenly highway.

I didn't get rid of the letter immediately; I let it sit on the kitchen counter for a couple of days. I read through it two or three times. Jeff appreciated automobiles, whether it was the Corvette he bought in his 20s or the Porsche Boxster in his 60s, he loved driving sporty cars. Every vacation we took, he would drive the rental car—over switchbacks along the California coast or through rainstorms in Florida—he loved being behind the wheel. He could drive eight hours a day, from Chicago to Kansas City or Omaha, and I was his navigator. Sometimes, Jeff needed no excuse to take a spin. He'd get in his car, turn on the radio, and let the rhythm of the road become his meditation.

And now, there was this piece of paper, thrust in front of me, reminding me that he would never need a driver's license again to enjoy the freedom of nimbly moving through space. Rather than immediately shredding the unwanted reminder, I let the feeling of what was no longer possible wash over me. I felt it was important to acknowledge and process the sadness that resurfaced from this letter's appearance. I'm so incredibly sorry Jeff isn't here to enjoy the simple pleasure driving gave him; the pain of it is palpable to me even now. Though hesitant in my resolve, the only thing left to do is take this piece of paper and shred it; a small burial for it and the sorrow that was its escort.

Reinventing Yourself

I was aware of the need to reinvent myself before Jeff died. We both had retired three years prior to his passing away. I knew retiring from full-time employment would be a massive change, but I wasn't in a hurry to quickly fill my schedule just because I felt anxious about how this next chapter of my life would unfold. And I had Jeff. He'd just recovered from cardiac surgery when the COVID pandemic hit soon after. We hunkered down until vaccines were developed, and the virus mutated into less virulent forms.

Initially, it wasn't hard to let the day unwind at its own pace. We could get up a little later instead of the normal 6 AM work alarm, eat a more leisurely breakfast, read the newspaper, plan what shopping needed to be done that day, and then go out together to complete our errands. Before you knew it, it was dinnertime. A well-known fact about retirement is that the day's activities expand to the amount of time you have. Eventually, you figure out an exercise routine, when you'll visit friends in another city, and so on—but accomplished at a more leisurely pace because the hard work over decades of employment has earned you this privilege. What I just described happens within the context of a relationship, and retirement becomes all about sharing the day.

And then, it suddenly stopped. No more sharing the day, an hour, or a minute. As a couple ages together in a loving relationship, if you have even an ounce of awareness that nothing lasts forever, you savor the simple moments. The best of what life has to offer is found in them. The loss of that effortless fulfillment is penetrating, and as obvious as it may seem, not easily identified. Sometimes, research can provide a surprisingly accurate depiction of how an experience actually feels, as when Neimeyer and Sands wrote about meaning reconstruction in bereavement. They describe that with an unexpected death survivors "can feel cast into a world that is alien, unimaginable, and uninhabitable, one that radically shakes or severs those taken-for-granted realities in which we are rooted, and on which we rely for a sense of secure purpose and connection."

People say after losing a loved one they feel lost, adrift, rudderless. For those who face this loss close to retirement, it's an additional assault on one's sense of purpose and meaning. The double whammy of two major life changes within a short period of time is daunting. One must try to work through overwhelming grief and figure out what life without their partner might look like. Retiring from a long-held position leaves you without the benefits your previous job provided—and I don't mean an income, insurance, or a 401K. Work offers many other things: it structures your time, affords social interaction, and fosters a sense of productivity. All that must now be re-imagined.

Jeff and I could've done a far better job preparing for retirement. The onset of COVID didn't help; it hindered our ability to explore or expand outlets for activity. But we didn't approach retirement with a plan—we just let it happen. I struggle with the lack of structure in my life now; I was so used to having my time organized around my work schedule and Jeff's. During COVID, Jeff and I were great company for each other. The imposition of a global catastrophe provided ample reason for not exploring pathways that might've infused more meaning into my life. The restrictions of COVID did have a silver lining—I got to spend an extraordinary amount of time with the person I loved most in this world before he so precipitously left. I wouldn't have changed that for anything. But

I still struggle to this day to understand what my game plan is and where I'm headed.

The term "reinventing yourself" sounds like a formidable task, and it is. I can't say I care much for the idea myself. How do I discover a new version of myself without my loving partner? It may require a different definition of fulfillment. I'm cautious and fairly risk-averse, so I'm not wildly casting about for new experiences. While I do give thought to the activities that fill my day, I'm also trying to remain open to what lies ahead. I sometimes get up a little too late in the morning and don't feel like I exercise regularly enough, but I try not to beat myself up over it. I'm doing the best I can to work my way through two life-altering changes.

Figuring out the "new me" as a retired person, without someone to share my days and nights with, is a gradual process of self-discovery. It will take some time, though I can't say how much. It's important to fully explore what has happened and acknowledge the effort required to figure out my third act. I don't have to rush to get there; that isn't how this works. How I feel and think about who I am and what I should accomplish will change as life continues and I have new experiences. To understand where I'm headed, I must do the reflective work as the journey unfolds. It will be okay if I take my time and be kind to myself along the way.

Everything's Okay Until It's Not

I used to say this phrase often to describe when an entirely unexpected event completely upends someone's life—such as receiving a serious cancer diagnosis, suffering a critical injury from an accident, suddenly finding yourself unemployed, or unexpectedly losing a loved one. Some of these events may be ones from which the person and their loved ones can recover. Other experiences have an outcome that is life-changing and cannot be altered.

In the past, when I said, "Everything's okay until it's not," those who hadn't heard it before would take a moment to digest its simplicity and the gravity it conveys about a life-altering situation. I recalled these words when I spoke with a friend who lives out of state. Elaine told me she had big news. When people say "big news," you're hoping for the birth of a grandchild or something to celebrate. That was not the case here. Elaine's husband, Ted, had received a diagnosis that was a precursor to the development of a form of leukemia. He could be treated now with chemotherapy, but there was the likelihood the disease would progress into leukemia, and the prognosis wasn't optimistic long-term.

Elaine and Ted are vibrant seniors, living well both physically and cognitively. I called them "little balls of elder energy." Then, everything was okay—until it wasn't. Instead of going to the gym or playing sports, it would be off to the doctors for evaluations, tests, meetings, and chemo, with all the fatigue and side effects that come with it. Suddenly, you're upside down, having to shift your frame of reference to what your life might look like, not just a year or six months from now, but right now.

The layers of change one must grapple with in such dire circumstances—psychological, physical, emotional, and existential—can feel overwhelming. It's impossible to consider all the potential life-changing events ahead, lest you be crushed by the sheer weight of them. So, it seems you take each day as it comes, marshal your resources, craft a plan of attack to fight this disease, and try to stand your ground. Holding steady is good news, every setback brings another set of adjustments. It's one step forward, two steps back.

When Elaine first shared the news about Ted, I felt as though I'd been unexpectedly punched in the gut and needed to stumble around to catch my breath. All at once my mind flooded with the possibilities of what they might be facing, none of it good. What robbed me most of my composure was the thought that Ted was ultimately going to die from this disease, and Elaine, Ted, and their family would be forced down the road of loss and grief with no turning back.

Upon hearing grave news, my first instinct is to try to make it better for the other person and lessen their pain. But I know my advice and solutions aren't what the other person needs, unless they ask. I want to say, "Do the simple things every day like eat, rest, talk, laugh, love, and savor the moment." But this isn't about me and the counsel I might give to myself. So instead, I offer that I'm a good listener and happy to talk any time. I won't wait for my friend to call me; I will check in with her from time to time. The important thing is just to be there, available and present.

***

Several months passed but the news wasn't good. Ted's pre-leukemia had progressed into the full-blown disease. Chemotherapy is never an easy treatment, with its myriad side effects creating, at times, an unpalatable existence. As cancer and leukemia become more serious, so does chemotherapy. Medical and existential decisions must be made about how to proceed at this point in the diagnosis. Your loved one must stare squarely into the eyes of a finite future and ask themselves, "How do I wish to spend the rest of my days on this earth? What do I want that time to look and feel like?" Families can hold a great deal of influence in the decision-making process. Nothing is truly knowable in these situations: only plausible risks, suggested probabilities, and possible outcomes presented by medical personnel. Atul Gawande wrote an important book on this topic, *Being Mortal*, in which he shares medical knowledge and relevant stories—his patients and his own—to give a clear-eyed idea of the forces at work as people face these critical decisions.

Elaine is a nurse and was involved in hospice care later in her career. She had a better understanding than most of what end-of-life choices are like. But knowing about disease, hospice care, and end-of-life choices is one thing; personally living through the experience is quite another. In the end, all of the available alternatives and life-affecting decisions must be processed by the one who is afflicted—it is their journey.

Ted's health continued to decline, and the prognosis was poor. But still, he struggled with the decision to continue strong chemotherapy, which would make him feel weaker and sicker, for only a 50% chance of a few more months. His other choice was to discontinue any chemo and go into home hospice care. After a brief hospitalization for internal bleeding, he chose hospice care. Ted died a week later at home with family by his side.

What the bereaved will experience after a loved one passes is completely unknowable in advance. Elaine's initial journey into the grief process was not so different from mine—sadness beyond measure, routines upended after decades of being indelibly traced into our existence, and waking up each morning knowing you'll be spending another day without the person you loved so deeply.

    My own experience with grief, though singular to me, is common in many ways to the experiences of others. I now see profound loss in a way I never could've seen it before—if I ever really saw it all. I've come to know the intensity of this experience in all its fullness, depth, and shape-shifting. I ache at the thought that those I care about will face overwhelming loss in their lives. I feel compelled to extend myself. Though Elaine's situation has irrevocably changed, my focus remains the same: reach out, be her friend, listen, be present and empathic, share when there is a purpose, and bring greater understanding, perhaps to both of us. That's all I can do, but it's enough.

***

    There is one more addendum to this story. When enough time passes, things happen. After Ted's death, I kept in touch with Elaine as promised. We talked openly and honestly, laughed, and shared what was occupying our lives at the time. Elaine remained physically active, and at the age of 82, was still regularly playing tennis. When I told her I was writing a book about my grief experience, Elaine, as a former academic, journal editor, and now a widow, wanted to read it. I was flattered she asked and eager for her feedback. She was very positive about what I had written, and it encouraged me to continue working on the manuscript.

    But about nine months after Ted's death, Elaine began to have symptoms of fatigue and muscle weakness. She seemed to be getting weaker very quickly. It took a couple of months before she was officially diagnosed with an extremely aggressive form of ALS. Three months after her diagnosis, Elaine was gone. I didn't know how to process this. The love of your life is taken from you, and within a year, you succumb to a dreaded disease. My first thought was, "This just isn't fair." But life isn't a matter of fairness, is it?

Adventure on Joyland Road

When Elaine found it difficult to talk on the phone, as taking a breath had become taxing, I texted her. I didn't know how long she had left. I was thinking perhaps another two to three months. As it turned out, it was only a few days. It's hard to figure out what to say to someone who doesn't have much time left. I struggled with the words but this is what I wrote:

> Hi, Elaine. Just wanted to check in with you. I know things aren't great. Life can be so very hard sometimes. I think about you a great deal and that I am a better person for knowing you. It was such an honor that you wanted to read my book and all of the comments and feedback you shared. But that's you, an easy giver to others. You are the best, my friend. Love you.

I guess what I learned once again is that death rarely works by invitation—it gets to choose the time and place of your passing. My advice is this: always, always, always say what you need to say when you have the chance.

Section 6:
Strategies to Cope

After my husband's death, much of my time was spent thinking about how I might move forward—examining coping strategies I already had in my toolbox and discovering new ones. There are many means by which individuals constructively or detrimentally cope with traumatic events, based on their developmental history, personality, life circumstances, resources, interpersonal relationships, and other factors. The following chapters provide a window into my coping mechanisms. Some may work for you, while others may not. Because this level of grief and loss was previously unimaginable, it now demands your full attention, compelling you to deal with it in one way or another. What's important is understanding which strategies might be helpful and remaining open to new ways of coping.

You Have to Own Your Life, No One Else Can

This was the first sentence I wrote shortly after Jeff died. It felt important to codify, as I was feeling vulnerable and adrift. Jeff and I moved through our 30 years together like a slow, steady paddleboat floating down a river. It was Jeff and Lisa or Lisa and Jeff, and now it was just Lisa. I was married or intimately connected to a partner for almost 50 of my 68 years (counting two relationships). Moving forward or not was now entirely up to me.

I once asked Jeff if he could give every patient one piece of advice, what would that be? Without hesitation, he said, "Anxiety is inherent in every developmental phase of life. You have no choice but to keep moving forward." Given his specialty in child psychiatry, that straightforward piece of wisdom is particularly apt and applies to any stage of life, whether you're 9 or 99.

Some life changes come our way without warning, with no expectation of the event and no way to prepare, as in the sudden death of a family member or friend or an unforeseen medical diagnosis. I am no stranger to an unexpected, life-altering medical diagnosis. When I was 24, I was in my master's program in nursing. My first husband, Ben, was in medical school, and we'd been married for four years. We married when I was 20 and he was 23—young by today's standards, but this was 1974.

I took an uncommon educational path in the early 1970s. After earning my bachelor's degree in nursing, I directly enrolled in a full-time master's program in psychiatric and community mental health nursing. There were very few master's prepared nurses in the U.S. in 1976. The federal government offered to pay for my education and provided a monthly stipend. They saw the value in having master's educated nurses prepared to practice in the community. This coincided with the effort in the 1970s to deinstitutionalize care for patients with severe mental illness, leading to the closure of large psychiatric institutions and the delivery of psychiatric care in less restrictive community outpatient settings. Ben was finishing medical school, and with some parental support and side work, we managed to cover our basic needs.

Ben and I were so engaged in fulfilling our professional dreams, what could go wrong? Busy with school and our lives as a young married couple, I delayed getting my annual Pap smear for a few months. I was unconcerned—I was physically healthy, and nothing serious had ever been wrong with me. When you're 24, feeling invincible is part of the package.

But there was something wrong. My Pap smear came back with suspicious, aggressive cellular growth, the kind that's indicative of cervical cancer. They repeated the Pap smear, and the results were the same. A biopsy was scheduled to see how extensive these cells were—did they stay within the borders of my cervix or spread beyond those walls to surrounding tissue? In those days, people were briefly hospitalized for a cone biopsy, so named for the shape of the tissue removed. My physician's partner saw me after the procedure, assuring me everything would be fine, but before the suspect cells were analyzed. But everything wasn't fine. The borders of the biopsy weren't clean, meaning there were more cancerous cells lurking beyond what they had removed. We still didn't know how far the cancer had spread.

I was given a choice at that point. The surgeon could take

another wider biopsy to remove more cervical tissue and see if the borders came back clean. If I chose that option, my physician said if Ben and I had any plans to have children, we should do so within the next year, as it would be best for me to undergo a hysterectomy soon after. The second option was to have the hysterectomy now, which would remove my cervix and uterus, likely eliminating any future recurrence of cancer, but also sacrificing my ability to bear children.

And there we were as young adults, in the prime of trying to achieve our educational and professional goals, having to make a sudden, momentous decision that would affect the rest of our lives. Ben had always been ambivalent about wanting children, and we'd put off any serious discussion about it. Being in medical school, he had some understanding of the clinical situation, the options we were given, and possible outcomes. Ben was in favor of the hysterectomy and the greater guarantee of my long-term survival. Growing up as the youngest of three in my family, I never had much opportunity to care for children. I also had no feel for what my maternal instinct might be and was fearful it even existed. Having little sense of the gravity of this decision, we chose option two. What I lost that day was not fully apparent to me until several years later.

Jeff and I discussed my inability to have children early in our relationship. He was empathic and accepting but didn't try to probe deeper into the meaning of this event for me. It was 23 years past what had happened, and I believe he realized I'd made peace with it. I was realistic and philosophical about it; you make the best of the hand you're dealt.

Do I look back on this life-changing series of events with any regrets? The answer is no. I did my best given where I was developmentally, what medical knowledge and treatments were available then, and the influence of people around me. In my mind, having regret is reserved for acts where you knowingly hurt someone or callously fulfill your own needs and desires—enslaved by your passions, you act without a moral compass. Once a regretted deed is done, it can't be undone. Perhaps you can make amends, perhaps not. All you can do is learn from that regret and try to do better. But this isn't a decision I look back on with regret; I managed the best I could. And, as Jeff said, you keep moving forward. Through other unforeseeable, life-altering events—namely divorce and remarriage—I ended up with children and grandchildren. I consider myself a lucky soul.

The issue of owning your own life keeps resurfacing because humans continue to transition through various developmental phases as they age into mature adulthood. Transitioning into the next chapter of life can be gradual, occurring over time with some anticipation of the change and an opportunity to adjust—for example, an upcoming retirement, a parent who can no longer live independently, or a spouse diagnosed with a chronic, deteriorating illness.

An intended retirement is an interesting example, as it can have a positive or negative impact depending on what people do besides work when they're employed. Some have hobbies and activities embedded into their lives throughout their professional careers. Retirement allows them to expand their time painting, playing golf, gardening, cooking, volunteering, or whatever interests them. Others who enjoy traveling, but never had enough time to do so while working, decide to devote themselves to seeing the world, often creating a bucket list of places to visit. Our close friends made it their mission to visit every national park in the U.S., and they did.

When anticipating a life change, we have options for how we choose to plan for it. We can do our best to prepare psychologically and behaviorally for the event, or just let it happen. When we let it happen, a crisis of major proportions can be precipitated. Crisis-driven change is assuredly not optimal, but denial is a powerful defense that delays the reality of an inevitable outcome. But when a life-changing event occurs, whether it's retirement, caring for a loved one with a debilitating illness, or being given a serious medical diagnosis, we have a choice in how we deal with it.

What isn't optional is the physical and emotional toll that event takes on us. After the death of a loved one, whether expected with family members trying to prepare or sudden and without warning, the effect is enormous and the pain immeasurable. There's no way around it. Along with the anguish experienced when a loved one passes, there are decisions to be made—many small ones that don't seem so small, and plenty of big ones that are truly consequential, yet you are in no state of mind to make them. This maelstrom unfolds in a new, uncharted reality where everything, and I mean *everything*, is different.

While living through expected or unexpected life changes, adults can make decisions that are either progressive or regressive. These choices will profoundly affect how they live the rest of their lives. I can take care of myself in healthier ways or not. I can reach out to others or withdraw. There are decisions to be made. It felt as though I needed to put a stake in the ground and consciously declare that I was now responsible for fully owning my life.

***

Things are the way they were destined to be

I must find my way back to the beginning

Without parent or spouse to share the journey

By myself, but not alone

I must discover how to be, just be, in this world.

Accomplish Something Small Every Day

This was an early, conscious thought after Jeff died—and an important one—but first, I had to convince myself that accomplishing just one small thing every day was enough. That one thing might be taking a walk, going to the grocery store, or returning a phone call. It didn't have to be something big, or fit some previous definition I had for being industrious. The old energy wasn't there to tackle the long list of tasks I used to handle most days. Accomplishing one thing per day would be fine. So would five things, but five would be judged no better than one; I couldn't afford to put myself under that pressure. The initial weight of grief is a heavy load: your energy is sapped and concentration diminished. This isn't clinical depression to be fixed with medication. It's right-between-the-eyes, breath-taking grief that has its own course to follow.

Two weeks after Jeff passed away, I forced myself to go swimming in the pool at my condominium. I learned to swim when I was 14—a bit tardy, but better late than never. A few years ago, I began swimming for exercise; it seemed like a good idea for more mature joints. I joke that, for me, swimming for an hour is an exercise in trying not to drown. But I take swimming seriously and give it my all, even if being a water creature isn't second nature. I kept swimming all summer after Jeff died. The pool became a place of peace, refuge, and meditation for me.

I occasionally joined the ladies in my building when they went for their morning walk. At first, I didn't say much, but I walked with them nonetheless. No one had any expectations I would be my "normal" outgoing self; they just let me cruise along with them. I made sure I ate. I'm a three-meal-a-day person, very much a creature of habit. I made simple dinners for myself, not that I could cook anything sophisticated or elaborate. Poor Jeff had to bear my mediocre cooking for our entire marriage. I always felt bad about that.

In a way I never had before, I was diligent about calling and connecting with family and friends. I picked up the phone, met people for dinner, and engaged socially with a wider group of friends and acquaintances. As a result, I've developed new relationships and deepened existing ones. I didn't have some well-thought-out plan, saying to myself, "Heh, you need friends and relationships in your life or you'll turn into a depressed hermit." I just did it. In retrospect, I can see that connecting in meaningful ways with others has been immensely beneficial, both mentally and physically—it's one of the things that has saved me.

Losing the person I loved most in this world has been devastating, and it may change how I move forward and what I choose to do in the long run. I may decide on a different set of priorities that alters how I conduct my daily life. I'm the same person I was before Jeff died, but deeply fundamental aspects of my life have changed—chief among them is how I view the structure of time and what makes each day worth rolling out of bed for. It merits examination, reflection, and discussion. As a rationalist, I believe that the more I understand myself, the better equipped I'll be to handle challenges and live my best life. Both philosophy and science tell us it's vitally important that humans find meaning in their existence. In whatever way I now define productivity or purpose, if I follow that path, I can find meaning in my life and a reason to get up in the morning. And with a sense of meaning comes hope.

So, convince yourself—if you need to—that accomplishing one

small thing every day is your measure of having had a worthwhile and meaningful day. You're on the right track, having adjusted your standards for what it means to be productive under these circumstances. Pat yourself on the back for taking a moment to breathe.

Say Yes When It Feels Right

  I'm a born-pleaser. Let me take a stab at explaining why. I believe this quality, for better or worse, established itself from early childhood experiences. When I was growing up, my mother had episodes where she got "tired" and would retreat into my parents' bedroom. Today, we call these episodes depression. I recall there were a few times when my parents' family physician, a cousin, would hospitalize my mother in a medical unit for her "tiredness." She would stay in the hospital for about a week and then return home. In the 1950s, an attending physician could hospitalize a patient with little restriction from insurance companies. If you had private insurance, like Blue Cross/Blue Shield, they would pay the hospital bill, no questions asked. Amazing, but true, in light of today's highly regulated healthcare environment.

  Sometimes my mother would become angry with my father and similarly withdraw to the bedroom after she made dinner for the family. This could go on for days. I would knock softly on the bedroom door, announce it was me, and enter cautiously. The room was dark, the shades drawn, and my mother lay in bed, even though it was still light outside. I would kneel at the side of the bed and plaintively appeal for her to join the family again. I could tell my father was miserable—her absence put a pall on the entire family. My dad would try to coax my mother out of the bedroom, but that never seemed to work. For whatever reason I failed to discern as a child, my mother would eventually rejoin our family world.

Adventure on Joyland Road

As a child, you generally aren't privy to your parents' interior pain, nor do you have context for understanding their defense mechanisms. Even if you can get past the idea that this unhappy situation isn't about you, you figure you can fix it or at least make it better. My mother's withdrawal from the family felt like emotional abandonment to us. I did everything I could to please her—worked hard to get good grades, tried to be entertaining—whatever I could think of so she wouldn't withdraw from us again. This reasoning wasn't part of my conscious thinking then; I was just a kid. But looking back through the lens of adult knowledge and experience allows me to reconstruct how profound early experiences shaped who I am.

When my mother wasn't tired, depressed, or upset with my father, I did feel loved by her. Though my mother was wrapped tight emotionally, she hugged me in the warmest of ways. She would hold me close and hang on for a while, as did I, both of us needing the unconditional love shared in that moment. I suppose I was her safe outlet, being the youngest of her three children by eleven and seven years. She also lived vicariously through me. I see that now. My seven long years of art lessons (rather than pursuing more athletically inclined activities) and the push to "be a doctor" were likely tied to her need for personal fulfillment—something she felt she never achieved in her own life.

This is my historical interpretation, one that's still painful to reconstruct, as I attempt to convey why being a pleaser became part of my personality. I do recognize it as something I was prone, or perhaps programmed is a better word, to do. Not anymore.

In practical terms, I've always found it hard to decline an invitation, whether to an event, a dinner, or anything else. Early on after Jeff passed away, some friends of his invited me to join them for a benefit concert at a large public venue in downtown Chicago. I'd have to travel into the heart of the city, park my car and walk to the venue, listen to music I didn't particularly care for, and then return home late in the evening. Initially, I felt guilty saying no—these friends were doing their best to offer comfort. But the whole evening was way too much for me. My energy and ability to concentrate were limited. I had no one to travel with and share the driving to and from the venue (my eyes aren't quite what they used to be). Everything would feel different because now I was flying solo. I quickly recognized my limitations and declined the invitation graciously and honestly. Friends and family try to help, but they don't always know what you truly need.

Generally, I've found that saying yes to social invitations is usually a good idea. I probably say yes about 95% of the time. Jeff and I didn't have a hugely active social life. Sure, we saw friends socially, but the pandemic put a big dent in that. While we were working, socializing on weeknights was usually out of the question. Weekends got busy striving to catch up with household tasks and the need to relax and take a breath. Not the best way to conduct one's life, but probably not unlike so many couples who spend an inordinate amount of time building their professional lives (still no excuse). Besides, Jeff and I were great company for one another, always immersed in conversation and making jokes.

I also recognize that I am an extrovert and thrive on interacting with people. While Jeff was alive, all the social engagement I needed was woven into my professional and marital life. Now, I'm retired from full-time work and have lost my best friend and loving spouse. After Jeff's death, my personality wasn't going to suddenly change. What needed to be different was how I interacted with people. I had to develop new habits and deepen relationships with friends and family. I now frequently walk in the morning with the women who live in my condo building. Do we get some exercise, sure. But I walk with them for the pleasure of their company and companionship. Some in the group have spouses, others are widows, and some are divorced, but they're all good, kind people. I am grateful to know them.

Though it's been months since Jeff's passing, I still curate my day's activities. I recognize I'm fortunate to be in a position to do that. The lasting effects of grief and loss are not to be underestimated. Too much stuff, packed into too many days in a row, is more mentally and physically depleting than you might expect when you're grieving. This doesn't fit my previous sense of self, which was the "you're a tough guy, you can get through anything" mentality. I'm apparently not such a tough guy and have limitations on what my body and soul can bear.

I don't feel guilty now declining a friendly invitation, so I say no when it doesn't feel right, even if I can't immediately articulate why. I can no longer afford the effort of trying to meet the outsized expectations I or others might hold for me. I'm trying to listen more attentively to an inner voice that's in tune with my current abilities. I've begun considering myself as a factor in the "pleasing equation." This is a new perspective for me, a different way to balance expectations. I'm not quite there yet, but I'm learning.

The Kindness of Others and Compassionate Listening

Right after Jeff died, I was genuinely amazed at the kindness other people—family, friends, colleagues, patients, even people I didn't know—offered. I'm not sure what I expected: in fact, I had no expectations, since I wasn't anticipating Jeff's sudden death. But there they were, all these people showing up for Jeff, the kids, and me. These weren't just individuals I considered good friends of mine or Jeff's, these were people from our professional lives, acquaintances, and neighbors. Even a friend Jeff hadn't spoken to in years wrote a long, remarkable letter to me and Jeff's children, sharing what Jeff meant to him, the work they'd done together, and Jeff's devotion to his family and patients. Whether people sent a card, letter, or email, spoke with me, or brought food to the shiva, I was genuinely humbled by their thoughtfulness. I vowed I would never forget.

But for me, never forgetting is more than just warmly remembering. I must be able to do the same for others—be there for them with a word, gesture, or action that might bring comfort or lighten their load. It's important I don't try to "fix it" by anxiously proposing a solution that worked for me or others, or by sharing something I read. Instead, I need to truly listen to another's pain. Listening is hard, and offering one's own experiences too soon is a natural response when trying to help someone you care about repair their damaged soul. You don't want the other person to feel sad, depressed, or in pain. The motivation to offer comfort doesn't come from a bad place.

Sometimes, when friends quickly offer their advice or solutions, it's because they're uncomfortable and anxious about the profound effects and consequences of death. Whether the advice is well-meaning, or motivated by someone else's apprehensive feelings, it isn't what a bereaved friend or family member necessarily needs. A grieving person wants to talk to someone who is capable of listening, and the discomfort one feels in allowing a deeply hurt person to express themselves is part of compassionate listening.

I must try to remember to ask more questions, give less advice, and let the other person talk while I earnestly try to grasp what they are saying. Sometimes, being fully present and saying nothing is all that's required.

Jeff was a professional listener by trade. However, he didn't confine his remarkable ability to listen and understand another person's issues to his professional life. Sometimes, he was approached in unlikely places. Life is a series of moments strung together. What you make of those moments is up to you.

***

In the Moment

Jeff didn't shy away from helping complete strangers he encountered by chance. This happened more times than I can count, but some particularly memorable occasions stand out and often occurred when we were on vacation.

Jeff and I were delayed on a flight out of San Francisco after visiting our kids and grandkids. We were sitting in the terminal at one of those long, skinny tables with charging outlets, talking away as usual. A very tall, youngish African-American man, Ray, approached the other side of the table and sat down. He immediately struck up a conversation—where are you headed and did you enjoy your trip to San Francisco? It was amiable airport banter. But he soon shifted the conversation in a different direction and said, "You two look like you have a good marriage. How did you do that?"

Definitely not the usual airport chit-chat. I said, "Do you know who you just asked that question to?" I didn't wait for an answer. I smiled and quickly responded, "A psychiatrist and a psychiatric nurse." I then dove right into the elements of our relationship I thought made it work—things like communication, talking through conflict, respect for one another, laughing together, and most definitely, being in love. Jeff's tactic was to ask Ray why he approached with his question.

Ray said he was having trouble with his significant other, the mother of his only child. Ray was a former professional basketball player and described some recent rocky times with his companion. She was engaging in behaviors that were risky to herself and their child. She was, at times, abusive to Ray. He had recently met another woman he liked, and she seemed well-grounded, but he wasn't sure if he should move forward in that relationship. Ray still had feelings for the mother of his child and wasn't sure how to proceed there either. Jeff asked Ray a few more questions before offering his best professional advice.

This was a 30 to 40-minute conversation in the middle of a busy airport. Shortly after, boarding began for our flight. We wished Ray well knowing we would never see him again. Ray was grateful for the conversation and wished us the same.

Two things strike me about this encounter. First, Ray correctly perceived that Jeff and I had a good relationship. He could've chosen any number of other couples seated nearby, but he picked us. Second, Jeff immediately recognized Ray was troubled and didn't hesitate to engage with someone who was reaching out.

Jeff could quickly *connect* with people *authentically*, making it comfortable for Ray to *share* his situation *without feeling judged*. But Jeff also possessed a rarer quality. He had a confident demeanor that conveyed he knew what he was doing. He *asked* direct *questions*, the right questions, and then *truly listen*ed. Complete strangers allowed him into their lives and shared intimate confidences. Jeff *offered advice not with a know-it-all attitude*, but by integrating what he was hearing with a wealth of clinical knowledge, experience, and *a caring manner*. What a gift he didn't mind sharing with others, and what a valuable lesson for me to remember.

However, the bigger implication is that you don't need to be a psychiatrist to be present for others or be in the moment with them. The bullets below are a brief guide for anyone who wants to be present for another human being.

- Connect authentically
- Allow others to share without conveying judgment
- Ask questions
- Truly listen
- Offer advice appropriately and in a caring manner

The byproduct of selflessly helping others is one's own healing. The act of giving, with the genuine desire to support another human being, is reparative. But timing is everything in the grief process. When you're ready and open to being in the moment with another, the exquisite knowledge you've gained from living through a devastating loss will find its purpose.

The Good, Bad, and Trivial Moments

Jeff used to say to me, "You fight with life, don't you?" And I did. My need runs deep to have things go just as intended. When things didn't evolve as planned, lots of anxiety and frustration would arise. It didn't matter if it was too much unexpected traffic or too little left of an ingredient to cook with, I wasn't good at rolling with the punches. It seems odd for someone like me to react this way. I'm solution-oriented and generally figure out how to manage situations gone awry. I just couldn't control the distress that welled up before I figured out a new course of action. And then, the most out-of-control thing happened to me. Jeff died, and I couldn't fix it.

Jeff, on the other hand, did not get upset by the everyday annoyances of life. I suspect he was that way for several reasons. He grew up with a father who worked hard and never complained, even when he had anginal chest pain. According to Jeff, his dad would quietly put a nitroglycerin tablet under his tongue until the pain passed and not say a word about the episode. Reinforcement for being a quiet hero also came from the media. As an adult, Jeff thought it was important to be "a man," reminiscent of John Wayne's portrayals of cowboys in the Old West. You don't get upset or complain about the small stuff, as there are bigger issues demanding your attention—like saving the widowed farmer's wife from ruthless land barons or protecting your herd of cattle from bandits.

These silent, suffering movie heroes were popular when Jeff was a kid, leaving a lasting impression, much like his dad did. Jeff also had clinical experience with his patients every day, many of whom suffered mightily from what life threw at them. In comparison, getting annoyed with traffic never qualified as something worth becoming agitated over. What did it take for Jeff to get upset? When his car engine spontaneously ignited and caught fire while he was driving—that got his attention.

Since the day Jeff passed away, my response to minor, unplanned irritations is different. I don't, or at least try not to, get irritated by stupid stuff. Sometimes it's hard work for me to stay calm, my old ways so ingrained that they arise as an automatic default response. Other times, little conscious effort is required to remain composed. Maybe I no longer have that reservoir of emotion to waste. Or perhaps becoming annoyed by trivial situations now feels pointless compared to the gravity of what truly matters in life. As the saying goes, "Perspective is everything." So, be patient and don't get upset over small, inconsequential matters. It just isn't worth the emotional cost.

***

The Jack Story

There are some people in this world who, when confronted with a challenging situation, believe the least favorable process or outcome is likely to happen. If my plane is delayed taking off from the airport, I'll never make my connection. What do I do then? If my air conditioner stops working—of course, it will be a hot summer day—they won't be able to repair it, and I'll have to buy an expensive new one. This type of thinking, catastrophizing, assumes the worst possible outcome in a situation, even when there's no evidence to support it. A related idea is the metaphor of seeing a half-filled glass as being half full (optimistic) vs half empty (pessimistic). But these concepts aren't quite the same. I believe it's possible to maintain a generally optimistic, half-full outlook on life, yet still get bogged down at times by situations gone awry—catastrophize. I am one of these people.

I generally have a positive, if somewhat cautious, outlook on life. I don't think people are out to screw me; they're doing their best given their circumstances. I try to give my best effort and believe I can solve most problems on my own, or with a little help. Over the years, I've grown more confident in my ability to handle most of what life unexpectedly puts in my path. But I'm not perfect, and every once in a while, doubt creeps in. Not being the adventurous type, I begin to see more of the negative when the situation is less familiar, where circumstances aren't under my control, and I cannot be the sole agent of my destiny.

Jeff recognized this tendency and told me a parable, the Jack Story. He shared this story with family, friends, and patients as it strikes at the heart of how limiting and unproductive it is to jump to negative conclusions when nothing untoward has happened yet.

The story goes like this. Bill is driving along a rural road in the early evening. He's anxious to get to his destination before dark. There's no nearby town, just farmhouses dotted along the landscape every few miles between the corn and soybean fields. Another car hasn't passed by for quite a while. Suddenly, one of the tires blows out on Bill's car. He quickly pulls off to the side of the road. Bill has a spare in the trunk and has experience changing a tire. He's annoyed but not worried; he'll be back on the road in 20 minutes. But Bill soon discovers the one thing he doesn't have is a jack. You can't lift a car and change a tire out on the road without a jack.

Bill begins to think back to how he could've been so stupid as to have a spare tire, lug wrench, towels, and a pressure gauge in the car, but no jack. Ah, he thinks, when I cleaned out my trunk last week preparing for this trip, I didn't remember to put the jack back in. A lot of good that does me! What now?

Adventure on Joyland Road

Bill eyes a farmhouse in the distance, perhaps a mile away. He thinks it's a safe bet the farmer will have a jack and lend it to him. Bill sets off for the farmhouse as twilight begins to settle in. He's trying to stay calm but starts to worry that, by the time he gets to the house, it might be dark and he could startle the farmer and his family by knocking on their door. Bill decides this is his only viable option as cars aren't passing in either direction. He has no other good choices.

Bill is about halfway to the farmhouse and starts to wonder whether his approach might arouse any dogs or other animals on the farmer's property. After all, it's a rural area, and most farmers have outside dogs that guard the property from two or four-legged intruders. That could be trouble before he even makes it to the front door. Bill is growing more wary and apprehensive about the possibilities that might await him, but he has no choice. Pressing on seems like the only alternative.

Bill is now approaching the front porch. It's completely dark outside the house, but the porch light is on. No lights are on inside that he can see. Yikes, Bill thinks, it's just a little past 9 PM, but the whole family is probably already asleep. Farm folk have to get up early in the morning to tend to crops, feed animals, and do a lot of other things I know nothing about. I'll probably wake up the whole household, and here I am, just some dumb city schmuck who got a flat tire a mile down the road. But wait, farmers usually have guns, don't they? Of course, they do. They need them to scare off the same two and four-legged beasts if the dogs fail in their mission.

Our intrepid traveler, having made it through the yard without encountering any hostile animals, still fears they might be lurking inside the house or barn, just waiting for the right moment to pounce. Bill is beside himself with worry and anger for all he might encounter. He summons up the courage to ring the doorbell. After an agonizing minute, a light comes on in the hallway. The door opens, and a middle-aged man wearing glasses says, "Hello, son. How can I help you?" Bill irritably replies, "You know what? You can keep your damn jack!"

Let's hypothesize for a moment that in response to Bill's unfortunate remark, the farmer slams the door on Bill and unleashes the hounds, as he worries Bill is a hostile intruder. Exactly what Bill feared would happen has now unfolded due to his self-imposed prophecy, in which a person's expectations are the cause for their actions and the consequences that ensue. Not only is the outcome adverse in this particular situation, but future untoward events have a greater chance of being seen through a negative lens. The concept of the self-fulfilling prophecy was first described by Thomas Merton in 1948 in *Social Theory and Social Structure* as: "A false definition of the situation evoking a behavior which makes the originally false conception come true."

Bill created a self-fulfilling prophecy, in which his verbal and nonverbal behaviors would induce the very consequences he wished to avoid. However, if Bill keeps his negative thought process to himself and doesn't say something regrettable, the situation may likely result in a more positive outcome. The question to then ask is, what mental gymnastics has Bill just put himself through? There's room for improvement if only he can recognize the path he started down.

Let's now say Bill pushes back on his negative thinking, swallows hard, and says, "I'm so sorry to bother you this late in the evening, but I got a flat tire about a mile back, and I don't have a jack in my car. I was hoping you might have one I could borrow. I hope I haven't disturbed you and really appreciate you opening the door for me." The farmer invites the young man into his home, thinks Bill might be hungry, asks if he'd like something to eat, and mentions that the dogs are friendly and love to be petted. The farmer drives Bill back to his car and helps him change the tire. Bill got a completely different outcome—the one he had hoped for—that wasn't precluded by

Adventure on Joyland Road

unsubstantiated negative thinking. Does Bill change his behavior in the future? That depends.

Once Bill is on his way, he reflects on the encounter. "Damn, I got all worked up for nothing. I stressed myself out about all the bad things that could happen, but none of them did. The farmer was really nice. He said I wasn't the first person who ever came to his door needing help, and folks around here help each other out. I tried to think through all my options which was okay. But there was no need to think of every possible thing that could go wrong and assume the worst; it just wasn't helpful. Next time I'm going to keep my cool and wait and see what happens."

***

I've tried to take this advice to heart. Not too long ago my car was hit in a parking lot while I was in the car. It was clearly the other driver's fault as I wasn't moving. As soon as I was hit, these thoughts instantly flashed through my head: "Just great, the other car is an older model SUV, the driver's not going to have insurance or at least good insurance, she'll say the accident was my fault," and on and on. I didn't say much when I got out of my car, but I'm sure my face indicated I was none too happy. The other driver, Sarah, immediately apologized for hitting me and gave me the information for her reputable insurance company. Sarah said she'd inform her insurance company about the accident. I thanked her for being a decent human.

On the ride home, I began fantasizing about how difficult and inconvenient this process was going to be. The insurance company would ignore my calls, they wouldn't want to pay the full amount to fix my car, getting the bodywork done would take forever, and so on. By the time I got home and called Sarah's insurance company about the accident, she had already reported it. The claims agent was very nice and when we were done, I had a claim number and the name and phone number of the adjustor. This was on a Sunday!

Did it take time to get my car fixed—yes. Was I inconvenienced some—sure. But 95% of the negative outcomes I imagined didn't happen. As to the other 5%, I capably managed them as I do most things in my life. What these unpredictable situations require is first recognizing where my thinking is leading me, and then self-imposing a cease-and-desist order on my rising anxiety, which is trying to fuel this fire. "Stop right there. You don't know the outcome. There'll be plenty of time to get revved up later. For now, stay open to the possibilities. It might turn out better than you think."

Jeff had a way of helping people understand crucial life lessons through stories. My shorthand for this now is when something inopportune occurs, and I start down the road of anxious negativity, I'm telling myself a Jack Story.

Everyone's Jack stories—life events you hoped would've turned out differently—are worth a second look. Is there something else you could've done, or not done, to change the outcome? Is there a lesson to take away from the situation that you can apply the next time? Learning from a negative experience may not only improve future outcomes, but alter how you feel about the current situation. At the very least, you've uncovered something valuable that could change how you think, feel, or act next time. Everyone has their own stories from which to learn. Make the most of them.

The Virtue of Humor

During the first month or two after Jeff's death, I didn't feel like I had any capacity to re-engage with life. I was too heartbroken. I drifted through the days outwardly doing the "right" things to care for myself. Silently, I was just trying to make it to the evening, when sleep would overtake me, and I wouldn't be so aware of my interior pain. But I was concerned I'd never enjoy or be fulfilled by anything ever again, and if I did, I would be overcome with guilt.

Much of my previous day-to-day satisfaction with my life came from being with my husband. There were many reasons for that, but a prominent one was that he was the funniest person I'd ever known. Are there comic geniuses who are funnier? Sure. But I don't know them, and I definitely didn't live with them. Jeff was smart and creative, using those skills to make me laugh all the time. Admittedly, I was a great audience and a humorist at heart myself. I appreciate humor of all kinds, and there's nothing better to encourage a comic than a receptive audience. That daily patter was ripped away, literally, in a heartbeat.

My interest in humor is deeply rooted in my childhood. It began as part of the enormous task of trying to distract my mother from becoming withdrawn and depressed. As a child, your awareness of why you might behave in a certain way isn't all that sophisticated. You just know that if you do something and it gets a positive response, you're encouraged to keep doing it (a core concept of reinforcement theory). In my PhD program in the 1980s,

I decided it was important to choose a dissertation topic that genuinely interested me, knowing I'd have to dedicate several years of work to complete it. That meant doing an extensive literature review, developing hypotheses, collecting and analyzing data, writing several chapter drafts, submitting a final acceptable version, and passing a comprehensive examination. The topic I settled on was humor. If you're going to be married to the work, you might as well love it.

Typically, when working on a dissertation, one committee member is familiar with the statistical methodology you'll use to test your hypotheses, while another is knowledgeable in the content area. The methodology person was easy to find; I wasn't doing anything too complicated statistically. As for finding an academic expert in humor, no such luck—I was on my own and had to become the content expert. And so, I read the works of philosophers, psychiatrists, psychologists, comedians, and anyone else who might have something profound to say about humor. Sigmund Freud, John Hobbes, Norman Cousins, Victor Frankl, Carl Rogers, Theodor Reik, and many others found their way onto my reading list for what they could impart about the use of humor. I'm pleased to say that Aristotle recognized wittiness, or a good sense of humor, as a virtue worth mentioning in his *Nicomachean Ethics*. Even a Bible proverb makes an appearance: "A merry heart doeth good like a medicine" (Proverb 17:22). But the "something" I wanted to study was specific—humor used as a strategy to cope with stress.

Many ideas for research often start with simple, anecdotal observations. What I noticed was that if you hang around emergency room personnel (and they see you as one of them), it doesn't take long to notice their sense of humor. The jokes they make tend to lean toward the dark, sick, grim, or morbid side. It led me down a path to study the use of humor as a stress-coping strategy among paramedics. To quote my own study, the paramedics I interviewed shared:

Adventure on Joyland Road

Humor allows you to forget, to not obsess about the last call, to prepare for the next call. Humor returns you to a normal frame of mind. It puts the situation in a different perspective and changes your way of thinking . . . Humor allows you to go on to the next case and be effective. It may be used to get past a tragic event. Humor gives you a mental break.

My summary thought about these responses was: "These statements suggest that humor functions as a coping and defense mechanism, allowing paramedics to gain distance from, objectivity about, and mastery over a situation."

My dissertation chair and committee believed my work met the standards for doctoral work. The fruit of my serious labor was titled, *An Exploratory Investigation of the Use of Humor as a Coping Strategy for Dealing with Stress among Paramedics*. After completing this 200-page tome, I continued my academic career, but humor and I weren't done with each other—not by a long shot. I wrote a book chapter in *Nursing Perspectives on Humor* entitled "Sick, Black, and Gallows Humor or Are We Having Any Fun Yet?" When your colleagues find out you've written an entire dissertation on humor, you suddenly become a popular choice for invited speaking engagements at all sorts of professional organizations. Soon after I completed my PhD, I did 33 presentations on the use of humor in health care.

It's worth noting that a serious study of humor is like taking a graceful cheetah, running freely through grasslands, and bringing it back to the laboratory to dissect in an attempt to discover how it moves so exquisitely. However, tedious research about how humor works is *not* what conference-attending healthcare professionals want to hear, especially after listening to a morning full of dry clinical lectures. They want a little science and a lot of laughter. And that's what I gave them. I love making people laugh.

Jeff was a humorist long before I met him. He grew up in the Borscht Belt in the Catskills of New York, during an era when Jewish comedy was at its zenith. It was called the Borscht Belt because it alluded to the beet soup (borscht) popular among Jewish immigrants from Eastern Europe. In the mid-1900s, the Catskills became a summer refuge for New York City Jews who could afford to take a vacation, as they and other minorities were prohibited from staying in upscale New York hotels and visiting certain beaches. Old-time Jewish comedians like Henny Youngman, Sid Caesar, Mel Brooks, Milton Berle, Carl Reiner, Rodney Dangerfield, and even Lenny Bruce, appeared as comedic entertainers in the Catskill Mountain resorts. As one humor blogger described, "Borscht Belt humor is characterized by stereotypical Jewish traits, such as self-deprecation, insults, complaints, marital bickering, hypochondria, wordplay and liberal use of Yiddish. The Alter Kocker character type (a senior citizen with a Yiddish accent) was developed here as well."

Though the humor may seem dated today, those jokes won comedians big laughs from entirely Jewish audiences.

> "I just got back from a pleasure trip. I took my mother-in-law to the airport."

> "The Doctor gave a man six months to live. The man couldn't pay his bill so the doctor gave him another six months."

> "Someone stole all my credit cards but I won't be reporting it. The thief spends less than my wife did."

Jeff prided himself on being able to make a spontaneous pun in any situation, even if that pun was delivered under less-than-optimal circumstances. When Jeff was in college, he dated the granddaughter of a sitting U.S. senator. The senator was rather elderly and beginning to lose some of his cognitive abilities. One evening Jeff, his girlfriend, and some of her family, including the senator, were going to meet at Lincoln Center in New York City for an event. They had all gathered outside, ready to go in, when the party noticed the senator was

Adventure on Joyland Road

missing from the group. They anxiously looked around, but no one could spot where the senator had wandered off. Each one quickly moved in a different direction and began to search for him.

Jeff and his girlfriend soon spotted the elderly white-haired man. When they reached him, he looked confused and said, "Lincoln Center was right there a minute ago." Jeff turned to his girlfriend, and without missing a beat said, "Your grandfather has become incongruous." She got the pun immediately and wasn't too happy with Jeff; the relationship did not last. Though the situation may have called for empathy over humor at that moment, Jeff remembered that pun as one of his best.

Jeff collected many things, but what he enjoyed acquiring most was fountain pens. Collecting writing instruments has become a less popular hobby in today's digital world. Decades ago, these pens were highly valued for their beauty, and they wrote as smoothly as skates gliding on ice. When you like to write with fountain pens, you must also buy ink for them. I think I have enough bottles of ink to paint an entire bedroom in a rainbow of colors. One day Jeff walked into one of his favorite pen stores—yes, there used to be stores completely devoted to selling writing instruments. The owner excitedly said, "Doc, I have a new purple ink I just got in. You're gonna love it." Jeff quickly responded, "Nothing I write is inviolate!"

When Jeff was going through the most serious health event of his life, his cardiac surgery, he found a way to deliver a punchline at a most unexpected time. The surgery was long (six hours) and complicated, requiring several procedures to be performed while he was on a heart-lung machine. That evening, Jeff was not in good shape when he was finally taken to the cardiac intensive care unit. His vital signs weren't stable and his breathing looked more like shuddering. I could tell by the army of physicians and nurses coming and going from the room that they were worried about his instability.

Jeff was being artificially ventilated, as is customary after open heart surgery. When someone has an uncomplicated post-surgical recovery, the breathing tube can be removed in four to six hours. Generally, people are sedated when they're intubated; the tube is not only uncomfortable, you can neither talk nor eat. It was now the next morning, Jeff was fully awake, and he was still intubated. His vital signs weren't stable enough for the medical team to feel comfortable removing the tube safely. Jeff didn't protest. He understood why the tube remained, but he wanted to communicate with me. He started to make hand motions to indicate a question he wished to have answered. We then spent the next 45 minutes playing charades, with Jeff trying to get me to understand what he was asking. For the life of me, I could not figure out his question.

Somewhere around two o'clock in the afternoon, the medical staff decided to pull the breathing tube. I was so pleased about this milestone. I was perched at the side of his bed, waiting to hear his first words to me. He only had one. With a wry half-smile, he lifted his head slightly to face me and said, "Divorce!" I laughed pretty hard, which completely delighted him. And the question he kept asking all morning: "How long was the surgery?"

If you multiply the stories I just shared with the days, years, and decades Jeff and I spent together, that's a lot of puns and funny riffs. As I was no different in my desire to create humor, sometimes it became a friendly competition. But it was the best kind of competition, where smiles and laughter went to the victor, and there were no losers. Even now with Jeff gone, I can't stop myself from punning. I was sitting with my morning walking group at a Starbucks. One of the ladies said she had gone to a restaurant the night before, and her food was brought to the table by a robot. She asked the group rhetorically, "How do you tip a robot?" I quickly answered, "You give it a byte." *Ba-boom!*

Jeff was a versatile comedian; he was equally comfortable doing adolescent physical humor as he was being quick-witted. When I made pasta for dinner, he would inevitably take a mouthful of linguine and let the long strands hang from his mouth as he shook his head back and forth like a deranged Muppet, mugging for his audience of one. He'd seize an everyday object like a basket or a box, put it on his bald head, make a funny face, and then implore me to take a photo of him to send to the grandkids. He let the grandchildren dress him up in whatever funny costumes, jewelry, or glasses they had on hand. Some of my most memorable photos of him are in full-play regalia. For Jeff, it was all about getting a laugh. His widest grins were always reserved for his grandchildren.

Seven months after Jeff's death, do I laugh? Yes. Do I feel guilt? No. But I can't replace that special repartee between us. It was one of the reasons we got along so well and spent decades never getting bored with each other. Jeff could sit in front of his computer, reading some ridiculous story on the internet, and belly laugh out loud. It happened quite frequently. I find comfort in knowing he could still laugh with me at all of life's absurdities. I always try to think about what Jeff would want for me now. Without a doubt, he'd want me to laugh.

There's research that helps explain why our daily schtick was so important. Kiken and his colleagues explored two key concepts in the literature on mindfulness that are worth mentioning. People who demonstrate the quality of mindfulness are generally defined as being highly open to having a "nonjudgmental awareness" and paying attention to whatever is happening at the moment—whether it's pleasant, unpleasant, or neutral. We often think of achieving a mindful state through meditation or immersing ourselves in nature. But can there also be mindfulness in our disposition as we go about our daily lives, an effortless awareness and appreciation of what is happening right in the moment? The term, dispositional mindfulness, has been used to explain this phenomenon.

A related, though slightly different, concept from mindfulness is "savoring the moment." It differs from dispositional mindfulness in that it "involves responding to positive experiences with thoughts and behaviors intended to increase and potentially prolong enjoyment." Jeff and I shared a dispositional mindfulness that allowed us to notice and value humor in our everyday experiences. When we created humor from what was "in the air," we then could improvise, giving ourselves more opportunities to savor and extend those pleasurable moments. Kiken's work suggested that a person's dispositional mindfulness and ability to savor the moment predicted positive emotions during the study and contributed to lasting improvements in psychological health.

Adventure on Joyland Road

I'm not surprised by these results since the Buddhists were writing about mindfulness 2500 years ago. Buddhist philosophy also recognizes the central role humor plays in spiritual life. Though I didn't need validation from professional and transcendent works to affirm how Jeff and I moved through our shared existence together—and how I wish to continue—it does support our worldview. We were all about riffing in the moment, looking for comic material in the daily carnival of life.

Humor is deeply rooted in my persona, my life perspective, and the way I cope. More than once, when something absurd has happened since Jeff died, I've looked skyward and said, "Can you believe this?" Even though Jeff is no longer here, I won't stop trying to find humor everywhere it exists. It's my unabashed, guilt-free pleasure and a formidable coping mechanism, deeply ingrained in how I perceive and engage with the world.

The Enchantment of Nature

Pleasure is hard to come by when you're grieving. I worried I would forget how to feel fully immersed in a pleasurable experience again. But, then, there's nature with all its awe and wonderment. It implicitly understands the cycle of loss and renewal. And, unlike me, it asks no questions. Nature is a refuge, accepting all into its sanctuary.

I enjoyed being in nature before Jeff died. I'm not one of those in-the-wilderness types, going off the grid for a soul cleansing. Jeff also loved the beauty of nature and would go to great lengths to show me the picturesque places he loved. Yosemite was his favorite national park. We didn't camp or engage in strenuous hikes, but we were all in for the beautiful vistas and winding trails.

Now, I do like to take long walks with and without people to:

Soak in the sunshine

Feel caressed by a gentle breeze

Look deeply at how nature constantly changes

Understand the clouds

Be mesmerized by the sun-drenched trees and their streaming shadows after a morning rain

Spy redtail hawks floating weightlessly on invisible currents

Appreciate the rustling of crisp autumn leaves as they scamper across the ground

Adventure on Joyland Road

Revel in the sheer number of squirrels that live together peaceably with each other and us humans.

When nature wants to show you something, it requires you to be present and receptive. These enchantments of the natural world are sensory delights, small or not-so-small, depending on your perspective.

I'm lucky enough to live in a unique part of the Chicago area. It's called Fort Sheridan, and it abuts Lake Michigan. The name Fort Sheridan is not a fanciful creation, dreamed up by an architect or land developer to evoke images of a bygone era, where stalwart homesteaders defended their pristine land from nefarious characters—though that image isn't far from the Fort's true origins.

The history of Fort Sheridan is tied closely with two historic Chicago events—the 1871 Chicago Fire and the 1886 Haymarket Square riot. These events marked a time of civic turmoil and labor unrest in the City of Chicago. Many of Chicago's "landed aristocracy" were wealthy businessmen who lived a few miles north of where the Fort was built. They were members of the Commercial Club of Chicago, a group founded in 1877 to promote the city's economic development while safeguarding their business interests against a growing wave of workers striking over abysmal working conditions. These wealthy men had enough influence to negotiate an agreement with the federal government—by donating 632 acres of land—to build a fort designed to protect the "civic interests" of the City of Chicago from labor strikes and protests. In 1894, troops from Fort Sheridan were sent into Chicago during the Pullman railroad strike.

A military installation would also provide a barrier and protection from any disturbance that might find its way into the businessmen's residential neighborhood. None of the imagined violent scenarios ever occurred where the Fort's soldiers had to intervene to protect the homes and families of these men, but the Fort continued as a military base throughout the 1900s.

Lisa Rosenberg

Fort Sheridan is named after Union General Philip H. Sheridan, a renowned Civil War military leader, assigned to command an army division from Missouri at the site. Interestingly, Sheridan, known for his aggressive, scorched-earth military tactics, was largely responsible for establishing Yellowstone National Park—saving it from being sold to developers. He's the only historical figure with a military installation named after him while he was still living.

From 1920 to 1943, the Army maintained a major training center at the Fort for anti-aircraft fighting, with three artillery ranges along the Lake Michigan shoreline. Cavalry soldiers trained with their horses on the bluffs above the lake and along the Lake Michigan beach. Soldiers training on the beach occasionally fired ammunition at small pilotless planes flown over Lake Michigan. (The thought of live munitions being discharged around the Fort does give one pause for thought, especially since some have washed up on shore or been uncovered in nearby ravines.)

Troops trained at Fort Sheridan have been sent into combat in numerous wars. The first fighting unit from Fort Sheridan to be activated in wartime was the 4th Infantry, sent to Cuba in 1898 to fight in the Spanish-American War. The Fort's hospital was expanded during World War I to become the largest base hospital in the U.S. at the time. At the end of the First World War in 1918, over 60,000 patients were treated at Fort Sheridan, including recovering soldiers and civilians suffering from the great flu pandemic. The hospital is the only original building that no longer remains on the Fort Sheridan site.

During World War II, Fort Sheridan functioned as a Reception and Separation Center, providing information and services for troops transitioning into or out of the military. The Fort also assumed the operation of German prisoner-of-war camps located in the Midwest during WWII. From 1955 to 1963, during the Cold War era, the Fort served as a NIKE missile launch site. As late as the early 1990s, active-duty personnel and reservists were trained and deployed from Fort

Sheridan during the Gulf War. The Fort was officially closed as a military base by the Department of Defense in 1993. An Army Reserve campus still exists just north of the Fort, as does active military housing to the south.

Today, Fort Sheridan is home to 500 private residences that now occupy the land of what was once the functioning military base. Many of the homes are original to the Fort's early years, dating back to the late 1800s and early 1900s. A two-block-long barracks, its historic tower built in 1891, stables, a drill hall, a bakery, spacious duplexes and homes for officers and their families, a two-story officer's bachelor quarters, and the large, lavish homes of commanding officers still exist—though their interiors have been gutted and modernized. General George Patton had a short stint living at the Fort in one of the duplexes. The original Fort parade ground was a 54-acre savannah occupying the center of the Fort. Today, that land remains a natural habitat where dogs frolic and Canadian geese visit. With all its fluctuations and fluidity, nature in the Fort co-exists in a space where historical reminders still bear witness to a long, turbulent, yet now silent, piece of military history.

Abundant with flora and fauna, Fort Sheridan is located along the Mississippi Flyway, one of the busiest migratory bird flyways in the world. I'm told that approximately 60 different bird species nest in Fort Sheridan, and another 140 species stop here to rest and feed during their migratory journey. Each year, avid birders spot various owls, hawks, eagles, ducks, shorebirds, sparrows, songbirds, thrushes, and hummingbirds, to name a few.

The ravines that cut through the Fort have an ancient history. For the past 4,000 years, snowmelt and rainwater flowing toward Lake Michigan chiseled out rocks and dirt to form the ravines of Fort Sheridan. The ravines are about 70 to 75 feet deep with their own microclimate: they are cool and moist, sheltered from the wind, protected from fire, and relatively shaded from sunlight. The ravines host 218 different plant species, some having specifically adapted to its cool, moist slopes, such as Solomon's seal, witch hazel, and red baneberry. The ravines provide a welcome change in scenery from the vast flatlands of the Midwest.

    What has always existed, in and around the Fort, is the picturesque landscape. Lake Michigan is easily accessible, and for us Midwesterners, it's as close to an ocean as can be found in the neighborhood. The rocky shoreline, natural bluffs, deep-cut ravines, rich wildflower vegetation, wooded meadows, and abundant wildlife—mostly in the form of birds, squirrels, chipmunks, and insects, with an occasional deer, fox, and coyote thrown in—make for a mind and soul-soothing sensory experience.

    My greatest pleasure in life, my relationship with my husband, no longer exists. But there are other meaningful pleasures to be found every day. All I need to do is walk out my front door, and nature is there, waiting to wrap me up and embrace me with her healing charm and no-nonsense attitude. When I return from a long walk, nothing in my outer reality has changed, but I'm calmer inside for letting nature envelop me and show me her beauty in the smallest ways. For me, it's magic.

The historic Fort Sheridan Barracks tower

Lisa Rosenberg

Statue of Union General Philip H. Sheridan on the parade grounds

The beauty of the Fort after a fresh snowfall

The Unexpected Silence

The silence is unforeseen and stunning. Very early on, my friend Kate told me "the silence" was startling and unsettling. I thought she meant that friends and family would begin to call less often as time passed, their solicitousness waning while their steady lives moved on, and mine was still struggling to find solid ground. What she actually meant was much more literal. The loss of the everyday patter with your loved one has a substantial impact, and at first, is shocking.

I used to come home from work saying I didn't want to talk to one more person that day. I felt like I talked all day long, interacting with people non-stop. I just wanted some peace and quiet. Now, the silence is so loud, it's deafening. It is the dog whistle of grief—only you can hear it, no one else—and the silence doesn't bring peace, only a reminder of what's not there.

You don't give much thought to the sounds generated by the sheer movement of another human being when they are near. But when those noises aren't there anymore, along with the person who made them, you're immediately struck by the stillness the moment you walk through the front door. No rustling of papers, running the faucet, coughing, making fun of the ads on TV, or laughing at the comical thing you just said.

Laughing heartily out loud—full-throated, boisterous, and unapologetic—is not something people do very often. Jeff laughed like that frequently in our home. He could be watching TV or looking at something on his computer, and suddenly, I'd hear a deep roar of laughter. (I'd have to crack a particularly good joke to get that response myself, God knows I tried.) I think I miss the sound of Jeff's laughter the most.

With his marvelously deep speaking voice, Jeff was a disc jockey for a time at his college radio station. They loved the timbre of his voice but not his New York accent. Before they let him broadcast, he was told, "Lose the accent," and he did. Jeff didn't have a discernible New York accent when I met him except for a few words. I would tease him that the word orange wasn't pronounced "are-ange," nor was horrible "harrible." After a while, though, I started saying "*harrible*" too.

Jeff's beautiful baritone, unfortunately, did not make him a good singer. He was pretty bad at carrying a tune, but that didn't stop him. Jeff had a surprisingly vast repertoire of songs he could belt out from the 40s, 50s, and 60s, and he did whenever they came on the radio. If something from the day upset me and lingered into bedtime, he'd lovingly serenade me with a calming blend of lullabies he knew—it was so unbelievably sweet. I didn't care about the melody being off-key, nor did it matter that a lullaby didn't solve some real or imagined problem I might've had. I'd begin to breathe easier and feel comforted when he sang that improvised song. I even requested it on occasion.

Other times, when Jeff was asleep, I'd listen for the sound of his breath. One of my fears when he was alive was that he would die in his sleep. It unnerves me now, and my heart skips a beat to think that's exactly what happened. I would lie beside him in bed, listening for his inhale and exhale, watching for the rise and fall of his chest. If I were awake and out of bed while he was still asleep, I'd go to his bedside and stand close to his face to hear the sound of his breath. Though I thought I was being quiet, sometimes people can sense the presence of another and awaken, startled. That happened sometimes, scaring the shit out of him and me. Jeff would joke that I was like a wolf standing over him, preparing for its next meal.

I listened to music much more when I was younger, but then drifted away from it. Now, I often listen to music when the TV isn't on. The silence is so loud that I need to drown it out. I frequently tune into a streaming Sinatra station. It wasn't my taste in music when I was younger—big Grateful Dead fan here—but now, I crave the love songs. I find them soothing.

I know some songs, particularly love songs that couples share as "their song," can be emotional triggers; it's the one caveat about music. No matter how much time has passed, those songs that were special to a relationship can instantly turn people into a puddle of tears. Jeff and I didn't have "our song," so I've avoided that weepy experience. There's still plenty of music with titles like, *There Will Be Another Spring* and *So Easy to Remember, So Hard to Forget*, that take on a more poignant meaning, as the lyrics give my thoughts and feelings tangible form and substance. Some songs about a lost love can feel melancholy. But the ones that remind you of the beauty of your great love—well, there's solace in knowing you experienced that in your lifetime. And *There Will Be Another Spring* offers a glimmer of hope that if our loved one can wait for us, we'll be reunited to sing and dance and laugh with them again.

I highly recommend listening to music to calm your mind, alter your mood, give palpable expression to your internal voice, and most importantly, break up the silence.

I Can Do Anything If I Want To (Within Reason)

I can do anything and fail. I can do anything and be successful. *But I can do.* Over the years I repeatedly told myself, "I can do anything." It never stuck. I'm not a risk-taker by nature. Perhaps I was in my intimate relationships, which is odd in retrospect, considering the heavy emotional price one can pay for throwing caution to the wind. But things generally worked out there. I made a few mistakes along the way, but nothing that left a lasting mark. However, I'm not a big risk-taker in any other way. I've had a reasonably successful professional life. My self-esteem and my identity about who I am are solid. Yet, I've been reluctant to risk failure.

The best risk I ever took was meeting a bald, middle-aged Jewish psychiatrist on a blind date at a nice restaurant and allowing him into my life after a painful divorce. Still, I took some time to commit to marrying Jeff, even after Jeff, Todd, and I had all moved in together. I'd been deeply hurt by my divorce and needed to take some time to re-develop trust in myself—that I was capable of making a good decision—before I pushed all my chips onto the table.

Doing things you've never done before confronts you in all sorts of ways after losing a partner. When Jeff and I were together, so many things seemed to get done automatically that I took for granted just how it all happened. But it's not true that it was automatic; it takes time to figure out the reciprocity in a relationship and determine who does what to make life more pleasurable and efficient together. When there are two of you, one person is often better at something than the other, or one hates doing a certain task while your partner doesn't mind—or at least dislikes it less—or one isn't as physically capable of a task that requires strength or skill.

Jeff was handy around the house, certainly stronger than me, and liked to diagnose and fix most things that broke. Flickering lights, a clogged drain, and stereo and TV wiring were all in his wheelhouse. Because I handled many things in our marriage—personal finances, shopping, laundry, cooking badly—Jeff felt good about his contributions where he had greater prowess. I'm grateful now I paid attention when Jeff fixed things around the house; it gave me the confidence to try to replicate what he did. For the most part, I've been successful and feel good about believing I can give it a go.

Another thing I did in our marriage was planning trips and making all the reservations for airfare, hotels, and rental cars. I detested making those plans, but I was too much of a control freak not to. The payoff was I got to go on vacation with my husband and spend time with him. It didn't matter to me where we were going as the destination wasn't the prize; it was the ability for both of us to get away from work and enjoy relaxing and being with each other. Now I'm faced with determining how to go on vacation without him. I'll eventually figure that out. The right circumstance will present itself, and I won't be able to come up with a reason to say no, even if I feel uneasy about going. Not exactly a proactive strategy, but I refuse to beat myself up over it.

All the thoughts, realizations, and insights in this book struck me not as a fleeting awareness, passing through my mind like sand through an hourglass, but as something I felt deeply, physically. I risked paying attention to my feelings and examining them, even if I wasn't sure what might run out from beneath one of those emotional rocks when I turned it over. I felt my resolve harden—to see what was there, believing I could take the chance and not fall apart when some previously unobserved truth revealed itself.

It might be a good habit to remind myself daily that "I can do anything." It'll be tough to hold on to, but right now, I like that it makes me feel more potent—even if I've done nothing out of the ordinary. But I am doing something out of the ordinary, like so many others who have lost a precious loved one. I'm living through the worst thing that has ever happened to me, in the best way I know how.

I've often said the following two sentences to myself, and they bear repeating: *Just because you haven't met a challenge like this before doesn't mean you can't rise to meet it. Don't lose your confidence.*

***

Raider Nation

Like me, I never thought Jeff was much of a risk-taker, but I might've been wrong. I always considered risk-taking to mean taking big risks, like changing jobs or moving to another state. But Jeff took risks in less discernible ways. The story below illustrates how risk and challenge sometimes find you when you least expect it. What you do in that moment defines who you are.

It was on Jeff's bucket list to go to an Oakland Raiders football game when the Raiders were still in Oakland, CA and playing at the Oakland-Alameda Coliseum. The Raiders played their last game at the Coliseum in 2019 and then moved to Las Vegas, becoming the Las Vegas Raiders.

Going to a Raider's game at the Coliseum had the reputation of being an over-the-top experience. The main attraction was not the team, as the team wasn't particularly good then. From 2003 to 2015, the Raiders had some remarkably abysmal seasons, finishing no better than an 8-8 win/loss record during that time. But the fans were another story. Going to an Oakland Raiders game was like celebrating

Halloween at a professional football game. Fans, not just a few, would costume up lavishly and ghoulishly for the game. Lots of fans around the NFL dress up for games, but in our minds, Raiders fans were the elite of the pack.

Since Jeff and I both loved football, getting tickets to a game while visiting family in the San Francisco/Oakland area was an easy decision. And, as the Raiders were playing the Carolina Panthers, another bottom-feeder team at the time, getting decent tickets wasn't a problem. It was a memorable game for reasons I could not foresee.

We took public transportation, the BART, to the game. It was a gorgeous day—the temperature was around 75 degrees, with not a cloud in the sky. As we walked from the train station to the stadium, though the neighborhood wasn't bad, I knew we were not in a better part of town. It had a grittier feel, with graffiti adorning walls and sidewalks here and there. To add to the atmosphere, as we got closer to the stadium, we crossed over a bridge with a high chain link fence on either side. If I were a betting person, I would've wagered this was not a stadium offering sushi and vegan burgers.

We got to the Coliseum early, eager to take our seats and soak in the whole experience. As promised, the Raider's most ardent fans—Darth Vadar, Gorilla Rilla, the Violator, various pirates, and countless people with painted faces—inhabited the "Black Hole" and were dressed to the nines. They were a little scary in person, as we likened their enthusiasm to people who found their inner child after overdosing on caffeine.

Up in one corner of the stadium, there was a giant torch. The Raiders have a tradition that before every game the team and fans pay tribute to Al Davis by lighting a memorial torch in his honor. Davis was the Raiders' long-time owner, Pro Football Hall of Fame inductee, and American Football League Coach of the Year and Commissioner. The Raiders began this tradition in 2011, after Davis's death, and continue it to this day. Al Davis profoundly influenced professional

Adventure on Joyland Road

football and is revered by the Raider Nation. A celebrity or retired sports figure is usually given the honor of lighting the torch for each game. Experiencing this in the Oakland Coliseum was pretty cool.

When we took our seats, Jeff sat on my left. Seated to my right was a young Hispanic man, Ruben. He was amiable and talkative, and we struck up a conversation. Ruben asked where we lived. I said my husband and I were from Chicago and were visiting our kids, who lived in the Oakland area. He then asked about team allegiance. Without a thought, I said, "I'm a Bears fan." Jeff winced a little, thinking our current surroundings might dictate a more politically, sports-correct answer. Ruben was okay with that. The three of us talked on and off throughout the game, which was poorly played by both teams.

I noticed that Ruben could drink an awful lot of beer in a short amount of time; the cups were piling up. I didn't count them, but it seemed he must've consumed at least eight to ten beers by the end of the third quarter. I hadn't fathomed that a human being could hold that much liquid in a single sitting.

Ruben wasn't dressed in costume or vociferously cheering, even though he was a Raider fan; he was pretty laid-back. However, a young man named John, seated in front of Jeff, was more into the game—especially when Oakland showed signs of life. He stood up when Oakland finally scored and cheered loudly, encouraging his local seatmates to do the same. John jumped up again and shouted raucously when the Raiders scored in the fourth quarter. He looked around and demanded others do the same. Like Ruben, he may have also consumed a large quantity of alcohol.

John wasn't too interested in having Jeff and me abide by his request, but he knew Ruben was a Raiders fan and demanded that he rise from his seat and cheer. Ruben wasn't about to comply, and things started to get tense. Neither young man wanted to back down, and the war of words escalated. John leaned toward Ruben, jawing at him, while Ruben grew increasingly agitated. The verbal confrontation was on the verge of a physical altercation. That's when Jeff stepped in. He leaned across me and said to Ruben, "Look, this isn't worth going to jail over." Ruben replied he didn't care if he went to jail; he wasn't going to take any crap from this guy. Because Jeff leaned across me, talking directly to Ruben and getting between John and Ruben, it interrupted the flow of their angry words and some very negative vibes. Jeff continued to talk quietly with Ruben and managed to calm him down. John, whether due to a short attention span or having a few moments to regain his composure, started watching the game again.

Thankfully, no more scoring occurred, the rest of the game passed uneventfully, and the Raiders won. As the game ended, Ruben looked at us and said, "You know when I get old, I hope me and my old lady can be like you guys." Afterward, Jeff and I laughed about being called old, but took Ruben's words as the highest compliment. I don't know what other people would've done in this situation. Jeff didn't hesitate to insert himself in an uncertain and perhaps risky circumstance, believing he could forestall an impending fight. It wasn't his job or responsibility to step in and play peacemaker to keep two strangers from making a foolish mistake. But that's what the good guys do.

The Power of Friends and Family

During his life, Jeff taught me what it means to be a true friend. He had friends all over the country—from kindergarten through adulthood—he kept people close and didn't lose touch with them. He stayed good friends with Sam for 70 years whom he met in kindergarten. He would've stayed close with his other grade school friends had they not passed away before him. Friends from college, medical school, internship, the military, psychiatry residency and fellowship, private practice, and our neighbors all mourned his passing. I joked that Jeff could know someone for 15 minutes and be friends with them for a lifetime. It's such a rare gift.

And here's the secret to how he did it. It didn't matter if people weren't the best at picking up the phone and staying in touch, most of us aren't. We somehow think that if we contact a friend more often than they reach out to us, it's not a reciprocal relationship. We feel like we're putting in more effort and wonder if they really care, or if they're just tolerating us. Rejection is tough to swallow, so we avoid it in anticipation it might occur. A psychological explanation, social exchange theory, suggests that people internally analyze the costs and benefits of their relationships to determine their reciprocity. I asked Jeff about this because that's exactly what I thought. He replied, "It doesn't matter. You pick up the phone and call." I wasn't convinced.

Jeff would touch base with a friend or family member almost every day. It took years of seeing him make these calls to realize how people consistently responded. His friends were genuinely happy to hear from him, often ending the call with, "I'm so glad you called. Please stay in touch." Sometimes, the call would culminate in making arrangements for a dinner plan or a visit to another city. Jeff was no less conscientious in connecting with his family. He called his elder sister every other day and his children and grandchildren several times during the week. He talked to his nieces and nephew frequently. He was the paterfamilias of the family. At Jeff's funeral, his friends and family live-streamed the chapel service from all over the country.

Jeff's wit and wisdom made for stimulating—and often hilarious—conversations with the people he knew. What most implicitly understood when Jeff called was that he genuinely cared enough to reach out. The unspoken message was powerful: "I've been thinking about you and wanted to see how you're doing. You're important enough for me to make the effort to call." These calls, to be clear, were other-focused, not egocentric: Jeff wasn't calling to unload his troubles onto someone else. He was calling to check in, hear about the other person's life, talk sports or the topic du jour, and simply shoot the breeze.

As for me, I wasn't much good at keeping in contact with people. I had acquaintances, but few close friends. In my personal life, I had spouses who were my best friends and that seemed to be enough. I was Jeff's best friend but that didn't prevent him from reaching out to others. Though I resisted his lesson on friends and family, they finally took hold. Before Jeff died, I started connecting more with my friends and neighbors and got the same results he did.

Since he passed away, I've kept in touch regularly with family and friends—it's been a life raft in a sea of grief and adjustment. I learned from Jeff to get over the idea that there's risk in picking up the phone and connecting with people. *The risk is in not doing it.*

If you need more proof of the powerful effect of friends and family, look to the recent work of Waldinger and Shulz. Their book, *The Good Life*, presents 84 years (and counting) of research about what makes people happy and healthy. The single most important variable is establishing warm, personal relationships of all kinds— marital, familial, and friendships. Staying connected in meaningful relationships is key to keeping us alive and ticking while improving the quality of our lives.

The Good Life may be one of the more recent pieces of evidence to declare the importance of close relationships, but the ancients were philosophizing about it many centuries ago. In the *Nicomachean Ethics*, Aristotle proposed guidelines for living well. These guidelines form a system of virtues positioned on a continuum from deficiency to excess, with a sweet spot in the middle known as the "golden mean." Aristotle saw these virtues as characteristics that could be acquired and internalized through practice— giving hope to us all.

Aristotle highly valued the virtue of friendship as indicated in the following passage: "Being loved, however, people enjoy for its own sake, and for this reason it would seem it is something better than being honoured and that friendship is chosen for its own sake." Aristotle didn't have the benefit of modern science to back up his claims: no double-blind studies or endorphin levels to measure. Keen observation and a brilliant mind led him to understand the importance of meaningful relationships. Aristotle's insight has stood the test of time and the rigor of scientific inquiry.

***

When Jeff was alive, one of the best things I ever did was reach out to someone I hadn't seen or heard from in many years. And she wasn't easy to find, not by a long shot.

In 1989, I started working at the university, where I stayed for 30 years. The dean of the college, Dr. Kim Alexander, was the first of three I worked with over the years. She was a stately, charming woman who empowered her team to work collaboratively, without resorting to crushing micromanagement. I grew as a leader and was sorry to see her retire in 2005. Kim was more than my boss—she was a friendly, warm human being with a motherly instinct for us up-and-comers. I had a personal relationship with her as did others in the college. It was just a natural outgrowth of who she was.

Kim continued to live in Chicago for several years after she retired. She loved the rich culture Chicago had to offer and kept company for many years with a man named Jim, whom she dearly loved. But eventually, Kim's great love passed away. Kim became frailer as the years went on; she was thinner, more forgetful, and less able to care for herself. Around 2011, one of Kim's daughters, who lived near San Diego, decided it would be best for Kim to move to California to be close by.

I went to the Hotel Del Coronado in Coronado Beach, CA to speak at a conference in 2016. Coronado is right across the bay from San Diego. I thought it would be nice to contact Kim and perhaps arrange a visit. I hadn't seen or talked to Kim since she moved, and I was clueless about where she lived in California. I didn't know her daughter's last name either. I knew Kim had a son in Chicago, but I couldn't track down a phone number or email to reach him. I conducted every internet search imaginable to find Kim, her daughter, or her son—but no luck. I'd begun my search about two to three weeks before I was to leave. I was running out of time.

I began asking my colleagues at work if they knew where Kim might be living and how to contact her. Nobody had any information. For all I knew, Kim might have passed away months or years ago; she'd left Chicago in less-than-optimal physical condition. I asked my co-workers to check if anyone "from the old days" knew where Kim was. Finally, a few days before Jeff and I were set to leave (he sometimes joined me on work trips, especially to desirable locations), a colleague said she had some information. This person gave me the name of an assisted living facility about an hour outside San Diego where she believed Kim was living. I had trouble reaching someone at the facility who could help. I called several times, introduced myself as an old friend of Kim's, and asked if I might speak with her. Finally, someone told me they couldn't put me through, but would pass my message along to her daughter.

It was now a day or two before the trip. My phone rang showing a number I didn't recognize. I answered, and it was Kim's daughter, Denise. I was relieved to hear from her as we'd met a couple of times when she was visiting her mother in Chicago. But Denise didn't remember me, and she was suspicious. I wasn't expecting that and fumbled through explaining my long-term professional and personal relationship with her mother. I said I'd be in San Diego for a few days and would love to visit her mom. I could hear in Denise's voice that she was still wary. She said she would talk to her mother and get back to me. I didn't blame Denise for being cautious. Here's someone you ostensibly don't know, calling out of the blue to say they want to visit your vulnerable mother. I thought, well, at least I tried. I didn't have high hopes this was going to work out.

Jeff and I boarded a plane for California. I attended my conference for a couple of days, and then Jeff's daughter and her family joined us in Coronado for a few days of rest and relaxation. One of our family activities was a trip to the San Diego Zoo. It's truly a wonderful zoo, and we were having a great time with the grandkids that day. Just before making our way to the polar bears, my phone rang from an unknown number. I took the call, and it was Kim. When I said, "Hello," she responded, "Kim Alexander here," just like she always did when we worked together. She sounded as energetic and vibrant as ever. I was floored and needed to sit on the nearest bench. I asked if Jeff and I could visit her while we were in San Diego, and Kim replied she'd be delighted to see us. She mentioned remembering Jeff from several social occasions. We set a date for the next day.

After the phone call ended, I started to sob. My daughter came over to me and asked what was wrong. I said I thought I'd never again hear from someone who had been a good friend and mentor. But there she was, calling me at the San Diego Zoo, inviting Jeff and me to visit her. I was taken by emotional surprise at that moment, but in a good way.

The next day, my dear sweet husband—who had the directional capability of a homing pigeon (before we became dependent on Google Maps)—drove to Kim's upscale assisted-living facility in just over an hour. For part of the way, we traveled on massive 10-lane highways; otherwise, I suspect we might've been on the road much longer.

We checked in at the front desk when we arrived at the facility. The lobby was expansive and gorgeous, with a staircase that led up to a mezzanine-like landing at the top. Kim appeared from above, standing at the railing with a big smile and her arms outstretched, as if she were a radiant angel from my past, come to make an earthly visit and bless us both. "Lisa!" she exclaimed, as she began her elegant descent down the stairs. "Kim!" I shouted, standing at the base of the stairs, my arms outstretched to meet her. We hugged twice, because once wasn't enough.

Kim was no longer frail. She had gained weight, appearing robust and attractive as ever. She showed us around the facility, which looked more like a posh hotel, just with older guests. Along the way, Kim was gregarious, asking if we had any grandchildren and about our trip to San Diego. After the tour, she took us to her spacious two-bedroom apartment, the largest I'd ever seen in an assisted living setting. Tina, Kim's caretaker and card-playing partner during the day, was there to greet us. Kim said a former professional baseball player lived next door to her.

In Kim's beautifully furnished apartment, I noticed many family photos, numerous post-it notes, and no computer. Kim asked

Adventure on Joyland Road

again if we had any grandchildren. Whether she truly remembered him or not, Kim didn't ignore Jeff during our visit. She acted like she remembered him and was gracious in how she attended to him during our conversation. I stuck to talking about the people we used to work with and what they were up to, as older memories tend to be more accessible for people with memory loss. She spoke of her great love, Jim, being in heaven, and that she would see him again one day.

Jeff and I visited with Kim for a couple of hours until it was time to drive back to San Diego. Before we left, we went outside to the lush courtyard, and Jeff took a photo of me and Kim, our arms firmly around each other. Kim and I hugged tight just before we left. It was hot outside, and as I got into the car and took a long look back, I realized it might be the last time I would ever see Kim.

After I returned to Chicago, I called Kim's daughter to thank her for letting us visit her mom, and how much it meant to me. Denise was warm and effusive; she was grateful we had taken the time and effort to visit her mom. She said her mother was so pleased to see us and spend the afternoon chatting and reminiscing. We talked a bit more about what a great lady Kim was before saying goodbye.

I knew my friends and colleagues at work were anxious to have some information about Kim, as no one had any recent news regarding her well-being. This is the email I sent to them:

> *Friends: I was recently in San Diego and had the great pleasure of visiting with our friend and former dean, Kim Alexander. She is happy and well and living near family. She remembers many of you fondly and sends her regards. Though all of you may not know her, she was and is a lively and most gracious human being. Please see the attached photo.*

The outpouring of responses from my co-workers was wonderful and gratifying. So many people were relieved to hear she was healthy and doing well. I knew Kim wasn't exactly the person she had been before, but she was happy, in good spirits, and well-cared for by her family and the assisted living facility.

I called Kim's daughter periodically after the visit, but not enough as I think back on it. She continued to tell me her mother was happy and in good health, though her memory continued to decline. Then, in September 2022, we received the news that Kim had passed away. I emailed her daughter immediately to convey my condolences to the family. She wrote back that in her final days, her mother was as gracious, warm, and loving as she had always been.

Jeff opened my mind and heart to see that experiences like this are worth the effort for so many reasons. He was my willing accomplice, and I couldn't have done it without him. As Kim had hoped to be reunited with her beloved Jim in heaven, I hope I can thank Jeff one day for the gift of this memory.

***

About six months after Jeff passed away, I attended a family wedding in Florida. Jeff's great-niece was getting married, and I was ambivalent about whether I could emotionally manage the trip. The opportunity to travel with and stay at the same hotel as my son's family convinced me to go. I'm so glad I did, for reasons I couldn't have foreseen. Seeing Jeff's immediate family—his sister, nieces, and nephews—was a balm amid my grief. They were very attached to Jeff and wanted to reminisce about him as much as I did. Jeff had been looking forward to attending this wedding, so his absence was deeply poignant for everyone. Yet, we were still able to celebrate his memory.

Unexpected things happened, too. On the spur of the moment, after visiting with Jeff's sister, her son, Michael, invited me to attend a University of Miami basketball game. I said yes, and we were off to dinner and a game. It was a pleasure to spend time with him in this way. On impulse, I contacted some former condo neighbors who'd moved to Florida and lived about 15 minutes from the hotel where I was staying. I hadn't talked with them for quite a while, but decided to call anyway. Luckily, they were home, and we met for lunch later that day. It was a great afternoon of reconnecting.

After the wedding, my nephew and his wife, Jackie, were kind enough to let me stay with them for a few days, allowing me to extend my trip. I took long walks with my niece in the morning, had meals with Michael, Jackie, and their kids, and watched sports in the evening—we just hung out. Staying longer also gave me the chance to enjoy a family lunch with my sister-in-law, nieces, and nephews before I left.

A trip I was apprehensive about turned out to be a wonderful decision. It required me to risk being uncomfortable and emotionally unsteady, but my anticipatory anxiety proved unfounded. As a result, my ties with Jeff's family grew stronger. The last time I spoke with Jeff's sister, she said that when we talk, it feels like Jeff is closer, more present—like he is here. I feel the same way. Jeff's sister adored him, as did I, and she grieves his loss deeply. There's solace in believing someone understands the nature of this loss in the way I do. Family and friends provide sustenance that can be found nowhere else. Like the air we breathe, it is essential to moving forward.

The X Factor

Middle school algebra has something to teach us about coping after the loss of our loved ones. Many directions in algebra workbooks say something like, "Solve the following for x." But what does it mean to solve for x? Solving for x means finding the value of x that would make the equation true. An example would be $x + 1 = 4$. Easy, $x = 3$. It's simple math, and the right answer is obvious. The more complicated the equation, the more work involved. For example, $2x + 22 = x + 1$. You may need to manipulate a more difficult equation to isolate x, using techniques such as combining like terms and adding or subtracting the same number to solve for x. The more complex the problem, the less practice you may have in solving it.

When your loved one dies, there's a lot to figure out, in a practical sense. Some things might be easy, like keeping a grocery list and then shopping for the items; you may have already had plenty of practice—like solving $x + 1 = 3$. Other household responsibilities may be less familiar to you and feel like the tougher equation, especially since you haven't had the same opportunity to learn and master the necessary skills.

When Jeff was alive, we were a team when it came to handling household tasks. I took on more responsibility for shopping, cooking, cleaning, and managing our finances. That was okay with me. Though we both had professional lives, Jeff worked longer hours, seeing patients during the day and evening, and then he would come home at night to write reports. For decades, he worked six days a week and

Adventure on Joyland Road

many of those days were 12 hours in length. By taking on the majority of household responsibilities, I gained the confidence to learn and manage a range of essential tasks, including insurance and financial matters. While nothing earth-shattering, these tasks were important nonetheless, and Jeff trusted me to handle our affairs.

There were some things, however, where Jeff took the lead. He had an innate mechanical ability and an understanding of technology. Jeff was proud of his knack for fixing things around the house and wiring stereos, TVs, and computers. I was happy to be his assistant and tried to learn by watching him work, but this wasn't where my skills shone. I never had any anxiety when something broke or misfired in our home; Jeff was there to manage the situation.

And now Jeff isn't here, but stuff still breaks. This scenario has played out several times already. Whether it's replacing a hard-to-reach under-cabinet fluorescent light bulb or changing out the furnace humidifier filter, there have been all sorts of situations where I had a choice—either rely on everything Jeff taught me to handle these projects, or immediately throw up my hands and believe I'm no match for the task.

So, these are my options:

1. Let my anxiety take over and become paralyzed.

2. Remind myself I have the confidence to figure out how to repair or replace the object, and then give it a try.

3. Recognize that I lack the necessary skills and hire someone to fix it.

If I don't think I'm overmatched, I usually go with option 2.

Surprisingly, I've been pretty good at fixing stuff. But I also have been sorely tested. My condo decided it would provide bulk internet/Wi-Fi to the building through Company X, which required me to change service providers. Once the Wi-Fi was installed successfully, I could ditch a couple of cable TV boxes I was paying for every month and stream X's cable service for free. To do that, I'd need to purchase a new smart TV and a streaming device for an existing un-smart TV. I was anxious about undertaking this venture, but it was something Jeff and I would've discussed and likely decided to tackle. But no team approach now, just me. I'd have to solve for x on my own.

In my mind's eye, I pictured Jeff and me going to the store, eager to make the purchase, and then working to put everything together. I'd be confident he could figure it all out. As I approached the store that day, an army of one on a mission to buy these items, I was determined yet apprehensive. I bought the electronics and gave myself a day before setting up the new TV the following morning. But things didn't go as planned. I ran into technical problems I couldn't account for. I started to panic—I had bought all this equipment, given myself a pre-job pep talk, and now it was all going to hell in a handbasket. Recognizing that panic would not be productive, I calmed myself down and determined I needed technical assistance from the cable and TV companies. I worked at it for hours with the technical support agents. Finally, we got the TV working with the streaming cable service.

It's now mid-afternoon, and I've hardly eaten and haven't showered. The glutton for punishment I must be, I determined I must get the streaming device working on the un-smart TV. Things got off to a better start with this TV; maybe it was smarter than I thought. I followed the on-screen instructions and progressed through the set-up steps relatively easily. Near the end of the set-up, it asked me to type in my account's email address. I did, but the auto-generated instructions told me the email I provided wasn't valid. What?? It was the exact email address of my established account. I was completely baffled. With no next move in my head, I tried to find the vendor's customer support number online. Some companies don't make it easy to find their customer service number, and this was one of those companies. It took a while, but I finally found their number. Once I reached an agent, we worked through the glitch in their system.

By 4:30 PM, I had both TVs working through the streaming service, free from their previous symbiotic cable box relationships. My house looked like a tornado went through it, with HDMI cables, boxes, instructions, Styrofoam, and electrical cords strewn about. A neighbor stopped by while I sat in the middle of this maelstrom. I proudly showed her what I had accomplished, though it had been anything but easy. She asked me why I'd undertaken this misadventure. In relating the facts, I mentioned it would save me $20 a month. She looked at me and said, somewhat derisively, "All this for $20 a month?"

I can probably afford the $20 at this stage of my life. Her question forced me to examine why I persisted throughout the day, as if I were Don Quixote tilting at windmills. I've said before I'm a persevering soul; I don't like to give up or admit I can't solve a problem. That's my competitive side revealing itself. In this case, my motivation was different—I didn't want to give up because of my anxiety about tackling the job alone. Mechanical and technical issues aren't my forte, but I told myself confidence is half the battle. I always learned from watching Jeff because I like to understand how things work, and if I just hang in there, I can usually figure it out. And I did figure it out, with a little help. I don't want my world to shrink or have to rely on others if I can learn to do something myself.

I realized that day I couldn't stop learning how to do things just because Jeff wasn't there. I must keep trying to solve for x and find out what is true in each situation that arises. As I approach these tasks, I try to stay calm, look skyward, and tell myself to channel Jeff; he'll help me think logically and problem-solve. If I can do that, I'll keep building confidence to accomplish things outside my comfort zone. The goal is to stay as independent as possible, while also recognizing when leaning on others (interdependence) is the right choice. It's the essence of keeping a growth mindset.

Lisa Rosenberg

Going from a team of two, where reciprocity was built into that relationship, to being a single enterprise, is daunting. It's hard to comprehend all the ways that singularity takes shape. Anxiety and a lack of confidence can be restricting and constraining. It takes conscious effort to look doubt in the eye, swallow hard, and try. Trying is the most important part, even if you can't solve the issue. The famous behavioral psychologist, B. F. Skinner said, "A failure is not always a mistake, it may simply be the best one can do under the circumstances. The real mistake is to stop trying." And, sometimes, you may end up surprising yourself.

Section 7:
Philosophical Ponderings

I never considered myself a deeply philosophical person, but the death of a loved one makes you reflect on things you never expected to cross your mind. In graduate school, I was drawn to Irvin Yalom's Existential Psychotherapy. It made a great deal of sense to me. Yalom pointed out that the many ways people manifest anxiety and psychological distress stem from four fundamental concerns: death, freedom, meaninglessness, and existential isolation. Pondering death may seem like the most obvious issue, since this book focuses on the grief experience, but the other concerns play important roles as well. How do we make meaning from this profound loss? How do we confront the groundlessness that exists without our loved ones? If I am now entirely responsible for my life, what will that look like? In some form or another, these concerns surface into our consciousness not by clearly announcing themselves, but with how they make us feel. If we examine those feelings that arise from a deep well common to all humanity, we can begin to find a calmer place to exist within ourselves.

The Necessity of Distraction

Right now, and for the foreseeable future, most of the events that populate my life are distractions. What I do during the day—shopping, watching TV, exercising, listening to music, writing, consulting, cooking—are the things that draw my attention and distract me from my new reality. It's a reality I didn't ask for, yet the one that presents itself to me every waking moment. Therefore, I need to stay engaged with the people I care about, work that matters to me, entertainment, physical activity, and eating and sleeping well.

That sounds like the things most people do every day, and they probably don't think of these activities as distractions, but I do. And that's what they feel like because when I'm not distracted, I think about what isn't there—the banter, the touch, the laughter, the envelopment of the relationship. It's just too much to bear for any length of time. The activities of my life give me a break from the sense of loss that's become an undercurrent in the composition of my being. Sometimes, that sense is stronger than others, but it never goes away.

If it seems like I'm not fully engaged in the things I do every day or the relationships I have, that isn't true: I still give 100% of my focus and attention to them. Whether it's having dinner with a friend, sticking with a yoga schedule, or writing a journal article, I'm fully committed. But all of these endeavors serve a dual purpose. The primary intention, like that of most people, is to live a meaningful and enjoyable life. The second is to keep myself from falling through the cracks this loss has left in my heart. That is the conundrum of grief.

As Joan Didion wrote:

> Grief turns out to be a place none of us know until we reach it ... Nor can we know [it] ahead of the fact (and here lies the heart of the difference between grief as we imagine it and grief as it is) the unending absence that follows, the void, the very opposite of meaning, the relentless succession of moments during which we will confront the experience of meaninglessness itself.

The raw power of this revelatory truth demands my attention, and it staggers me. I move through the day eating, breathing, working, sleeping, searching, trying to find ways to feel vital, involved, engaged, appreciated, thankful, useful, or not feel anything at all. It is the enigma of grief. The days can be wearisome and long when there's too little to distract me, because a mere kiss, a touch, a smile, or a laugh were once the only things I needed to make my day. I didn't understand that then. How could I?

Hoping Against Reality

It's in my nature to figure things out. I feel a sense of mastery and control over my world when I understand how something works or solve a problem by thinking it through. But a penchant for puzzle-solving has its downside when you're looking for a little magic.

I desperately wanted to believe that an affectionate, saved voice message from Jeff had magically appeared one day in a text I sent myself, which contained a boarding pass from United Airlines. Jeff and I had been married for 25 years when he left this voicemail in the middle of a workday—it wasn't our anniversary or my birthday, just a day like any other. He said:

> Hi. It's your husband. I just want to tell you how much I love you, what a lucky man I am, and how much I appreciate you in many, many ways. Take care. Bye.

It was a voicemail I listened to many times after Jeff died. I wanted to hear his comforting, deep voice and the words he spoke one more time. Now, more than a year after he's gone, I find this voicemail nearly impossible to listen to. While photos may bring some level of comfort, they're static, frozen in time. But someone's voice—their words, a turn of phrase, their sentiment—can dance in the air with a life that momentarily exists. That juxtaposition with reality is just too hard for me.

How amazingly coincidental that this beautiful voicemail got mingled with a United Airlines text. United, really? The play on words did not escape me. At first, I couldn't imagine how I might have caused the appearance of this voice memo. For several hours I fantasized my guardian angel, Jeff, was watching over me and letting me know he was there. By the next morning, I figured out exactly how I'd managed to combine this voicemail with the United Airlines text message. I was disappointed by the confinement of my own logic. My attempt to believe in something beyond the tangible was once again overpowered by my rationality.

In those moments when the unexplained first appears, and I allow the whimsy of wishful thinking to drift into my consciousness, it's so seductive, offering a peace I rarely experience. When some event remains inexplicable, maybe you can ride that sliver of hope into the next realm and be cosmically "united" with your loved one. Wishful thinking can help you get there when chasing serenity. But figuring out every damn thing bursts that bubble every time. I'm a dogged, determined soul and can't help myself—it's just the way I'm built.

Besides being persistent, I'm careful and sensible, believing that as I move through life, I have some agency over things that happen to me. If I consider all the possibilities, choose wisely, work hard enough, and stay focused and committed, circumstances will favor me. There's truth in that. But it's easy to be blinded by one's success. Ultimately, death doesn't take no for an answer. You or your loved one don't get to decline death's summons, even if you vehemently protest: attendance is mandatory. And there it is, your tenuous sense of control taken from you as easily as sand slips through a child's fingers. It's replaced by grief in a shape and form you never knew existed.

And yet, while I cannot alter reality, I do engage in the fantasy from time to time that one day when I'm not breathing, Jeff and I will be reunited. I took a long walk on a particularly beautiful fall day. I strode across a wooden bridge covering a deep ravine. No one was around. I stood for a moment at the end of the bridge, taking in the autumn colors, the soft breeze, and the unusual peacefulness of the setting; it became an embracing sensory experience. As I looked back at the bridge and the path I'd just walked, the path curved around a bend, and I couldn't see what lay beyond it. Even though I'd just been there, as I looked back at it, the path seemed to lead toward some infinite space I had yet to imagine.

I pictured in my mind's eye that perhaps in the autumn of my life, as I leave this earth, I'd walk down this very bridge, and beyond the bend, Jeff would be waiting for me. He would greet me warmly and say he'd been patiently anticipating my arrival. He'd gently talk to me, and we'd laugh like we used to. Then, he would take my hand, and we'd begin walking together—side by side, forever. The tears came quickly as I stood on that bridge. I never know how or when Jeff comes to me, but come to me he surely does.

A quixotic imagination offers a captivating, though temporary, reprieve from the weight of everyday reality and the never-knowing of what lies beyond. It provides a soothing illusion when the existential nature of the loss feels so desperately out of control. When the pain is great, we urgently search for a reason to take our next breath. My breaking heart will not stop beating, being driven by physiological instinct. Wishful thinking winkingly promises a brief emotional respite, but it isn't going to alter that reality. It's too soon to have declared some profound, personal understanding of life and death that will offer a lasting sense of clarity and peace.

When Jeff was alive, I magically thought if I just loved him hard enough, immensely enough, I could will his body to live a longer life. Somehow love would conquer all, even heart disease. At the beginning of our relationship, Jeff promised me 30 years of being together, and that's exactly what he gave me. I told him 30 years was not enough, I wasn't going to make that deal, but he always held to that number. It was as if he were prescient about his longevity, but of course, he couldn't be. He wanted to live as long as possible, attend his grandchildren's Bar and Bat Mitzvahs, and dance at their weddings, even if his strength and energy wasn't like it had been in his younger years. But there I was, believing my sheer loving life force could sustain him. In the end, you never have enough time with the ones you love. Foolish me for thinking I had any real influence. Not foolish me for being so deeply in love.

> *"To be at peace with our helplessness is the most terrible and liberating of lessons."*
> Rabbi Steve Leder

The Crucible of Loss

I'm one of those people, like many, who has 10 thoughts going at once—what I need to pick up at the grocery store, who I have to call later, what work I need to prepare for the next day, and so on. As my mind meanders from one random thought to the next, I innocently put my phone down in one room and walk into another, leaving my poor abandoned phone to fend for itself. Alas, I've cluttered my brain with so many seemingly important obligations, I've completely forgotten where I left the most essential item for my daily functioning. What did I do when Jeff was alive? Of course, I asked my dependable spouse to call my phone so I could hear it ring. Upon hearing the plaintive cry, I'd run to my phone and cradle it gently, promising never to be so callous and recklessly desert it again. Except, I'd do the same thing the next day.

Now, I have no spouse to help me locate the place where I left my sadly forsaken phone. When that notion occurred to me, which was pretty soon after Jeff died, I panicked, as I had no great answer for how I might solve this problem long-term. In the short term, I still had Jeff's phone with an active number, so I could always call my phone using his. But eventually, I imagined I'd stop paying for service on his phone, and then what? Saying, "Honey, will you call my phone, I can't find it," was one more reminder of how I depended on Jeff to keep me on track. The small losses often hit hard, serving as reminders of the totality of all that will never be the same again.

Right after Jeff died, my daughter stayed with me for several days.

Adventure on Joyland Road

I mentioned I didn't know how I'd find my phone now that her dad was gone after I left it in some unknown spot in the apartment. She reminded me her father wore an iWatch. Jeff had always wanted me to get an iWatch, but I steadfastly refused. He'd say, "But it's great for tracking your daily activity!" I'd respond, "Do I look like someone who needs their daily activity tracked?" As I'm built like a spider and in good cardiac health, that usually ended the conversation. I'm sure he thought I was being a luddite, but at least I had a good excuse.

My daughter informed me the iWatch could find my phone. Say what? Just hit a little button on the side of the watch, and there's a picture of an iPhone with noise signals on each side. Touch that icon and your phone emits a few hopeful rings that you're dashing to its rescue. Voila, problem solved.

Another handy feature I knew about is that the phone can detect a hard fall and call 911 if you don't respond. It's one of the reasons I thought it was a good idea for Jeff to have an iWatch. But I realized I could benefit from that detection, too. I now live alone and climb ladders to change light bulbs and smoke detector batteries, and whatever else I think I can fix.

But the watch had more value than the functions it could perform. Jeff loved technology and was very fond of his iWatch. He enjoyed meeting his activity goals and would get up from his chair to walk around whenever the watch told him to stand. It motivated him to move, and he wore that watch every day without fail. Weird as it may seem, at least to me, the watch quickly came to have great sentimental value. His iWatch is the one with the larger face, running the full width of my wrist from the radius to the ulna bones; it looks like the watch is wearing me. Jeff had a lovely metal band for the watch which fit twice around my wrist. I found myself in the Apple store shortly after. I couldn't imagine living another day without that watch on my wrist. I bought a blue fabric weave band in a tiny size to fit my diminutive wrist.

Now, I wear the watch every day. It keeps me sane and safe, both literally and figuratively. I kept the same blue clock face Jeff wore. The display is the old-fashioned kind, with real numbers, a second hand, and the day and date. The face is gigantic on my wrist but I don't care; every time I look at it, I'm reminded of him.

The word crucible, as in the title of the chapter, has two meanings. One is that a crucible is a container or vessel. The second meaning of crucible is an ordeal or trial. I'm a person who has had a moderately successful life. I believe I'm pretty resilient and confident in my abilities, having overcome serious medical issues and the trauma of a divorce. I have a master's degree and PhD, worked in my chosen profession, and advanced to leadership positions. I achieved what I did through hard work and perseverance. And yet, I've been caught short by the sudden death of my husband. No ordeal in my life comes close to the challenge of this loss. Not divorce, not cancer, nothing.

Those who have suffered the loss of a loved one are the vessels that carry the ordeal of grief within them. The loss of a spouse, a child, or anyone you loved deeply, is all-consuming—physically, mentally, and emotionally. Some days you look for a reason to get out of bed in the morning; it makes you wonder if you can. But also contained in that vessel is all of who we are, how we choose to live with the loss, and what we bring to each day to find meaning. Whether we reincarnate an iWatch, connect with an old friend, take on a different job, or try a new hobby, we're moved to find meaning. There's no pep talk to get you across the finish line—it's merely a leap of faith, trusting that a core of strength exists within you to see your way through.

The Calm

Humans are hard-wired with a fundamental instinct to survive. Accompanying that instinct can be a healthy dose of terror regarding one's death. I used to have a sense of existential dread—a feeling of endlessly falling off the edge of a cliff whenever I contemplated my own demise. Now, I no longer fear "not being."

When this thought came to me, it was accompanied by a feeling of calmness. I needed to make sense of it. I'm not depressed or suicidal, and I wasn't trying to think deeply and profoundly about my death. The thought just materialized. My unconscious mind was working on something, and this notion surfaced into my awareness.

When the worst thing in the world happens to you, the fear of leaving a mortal existence and confronting the unknowable can dissipate—at least it did for me. It wasn't a conscious process of self-reflection that brought this revelation, but I could feel it in my bones. I'm calmer now about what I cannot comprehend, there is an acceptance of it.

There's nothing I need to rush off and do before the finality, nothing to cross off my bucket list. I've known great love, which I believe is the most important thing to experience and share. Psychiatrist and author Irvin Yalom wrote, "It's always more painful to think of death when you sense you haven't lived fully." Though I have a competitive nature, I haven't defined a full life as measured by professional success, being famous, the amount of money I made, or traveling the world. I measure the fullness of my life by how well I've loved others. If I were to leave this earth tomorrow, I'd have no regrets I didn't accomplish what mattered to me most.

Having come to some terms with the finality, I worry more about the infirmity that can accompany aging. Bodies aren't made to last forever, and they inevitably fail in one way or another. If you live long enough, they fail in many ways all at the same time. People want to live on their own terms, but choices can become more limited based on waning physical and cognitive abilities. Your children want to "keep you safe," but is that compatible with what you value and how you want to live the rest of your life? In the last few years of Jeff's life, he did have some physical limitations, but he was content knowing his mind was sharp and I was by his side. He didn't have the chance to become one of the frail elderly. Some would count that as a blessing.

I have several friends and family who are 10 or more years older than me. Some have already had serious illnesses. Since Jeff's death, I've come to develop close relationships with these people, and my fear is they will all die before me. It's a selfish thought that I'll have to endure the pain of their passing, but I think it nonetheless. My friends in their early 80s say it feels like they're attending the funerals of relatives and friends every other week. I privately wince. It's not my death that causes me angst, it's theirs. I joke with my neighbors that we need to find younger people to join our friend circle, but I'm only half-kidding. I don't want to be the last one standing.

I have no choice but to let each day unfold and reveal itself. I'm open to that in a way I never was before. Any pronounced unease about no longer existing in the physical world has abated—it's a sense of having made some peace with an immutable destiny. I hope that feeling doesn't go away.

The Grace of Gratitude

I said early on after Jeff died that I'm both the unluckiest and luckiest person, all at the same time. It's a fragile proposition. In tragedy, the worst and best of life can often be revealed in conjunction with one another. I've been lucky enough to have friends and family uplift me and experience true gratitude for their support. The juxtaposition of feeling crushing grief next to brimming gratitude isn't something I imagined would be part of this process.

Perhaps it has something to do with my expectations of people. I generally see human beings and their intentions in a more positive light than not; I think most people mean no harm and try their best. But I don't have any expectations of how people should act toward me or feel I'm owed anything. After Jeff died, when family, friends, and acquaintances were kind in ways I didn't expect, I was overcome by their compassion and caring. Though I was grateful for Jeff and often told him so, I didn't necessarily have a wide circle of others to which that sense of gratitude extended. But after he died, people showed up for me. It comforted my hurting heart and filled me with a peacefulness that was hard to find—I experienced a state of grace.

I became more fully aware of the instances when I experienced profound gratitude. I felt it when relatives from Florida came to Chicago for Jeff's funeral. They could've stayed home and streamed the chapel service, but Jeff meant enough to them to be there in person. Work friends I hadn't seen in three years came to the shiva after the funeral. Neighbors jumped right in and took care of all of the shiva arrangements. And then, there were the many letters, cards, calls, and emails I received from Jeff's friends and patients.

What some people wrote to me about him was extraordinary. These weren't "my deepest condolences" or "sorry for your loss" greeting cards, though, I did get many of those. These were letters, cards, and emails filled with heartfelt narratives about how deeply Jeff had touched their lives:

"He saved my life."

"The world has lost an amazing, one-of-a-kind man. He was in every sense of the word a true healer. A man filled with wisdom, compassion, love, humility, and a rich sense of humor."

"His commitment to his patients was unmatched."

Friends also shared what I meant to Jeff and how much joy our relationship brought him.

People's willingness to share their thoughts and feelings with me was exceptionally meaningful. As I read and listened, it reinforced how fortunate I was to have spent 30 years with someone who made such a profound impact on people. What also touched me deeply was how these people shared my grief in more than a fleeting way. In that moment, they wanted to think about Jeff as much as I do all the time. In whatever way their lives had intersected with his, these people wanted me to know how important he was to them. There was comfort in that—it made me feel less alone, and I was grateful for Jeff and the kindness of those who knew him.

***

Over the many months of grieving Jeff's death, my heartache has been intertwined with experiences of gratitude. I was grateful when people called and invited me out, appreciative when they sent birthday wishes, and thankful for happy memories I had tucked away. And I knew those varied sources of gratitude made me feel better.

For centuries, philosophical and religious texts have discussed the benefits of gratitude. But when I seek confirmation for my thoughts and feelings, my preferred source is science. In their book on gratitude, Emmons and his co-authors wrote, "From childhood to old age, a wide array of psychological, physical, and relational benefits is associated with gratitude." Gratitude contributes to improved happiness and health and has been shown to decrease negative emotions and problematic behavior. It's positively related to physical and mental well-being, life satisfaction, a positive emotional demeanor, hope and personal growth, forgiveness, self-esteem, sleep quality, self-efficacy, vitality, and subjective happiness. Gratitude was also found to mitigate general anxiety, depression, high-risk behaviors, and suicidal ideation.

If that exhaustive inventory wasn't enough to convince you of the value of feeling gratitude, there is a whole set of studies about the correlation of grief to gratitude. In their work, Elfers and his colleagues describe grief as "an emotional experience that touches every dimension of life. It shows up in the body, overwhelms cognition, impacts relationships, and potentially fractures the spirit." So, how do grief and gratitude connect? The authors propose a link between resilience in coping with grief and the development of gratitude. Their findings suggest that actively experiencing gratitude can positively affect one's attitude, emotions, and ability to find meaning—potentially building resilience and personal growth during the grief process.

The research implies one can cultivate a sense of gratitude if you are open to it. It can be found in the simplest gestures others extend to you. A young man, my neighbor's son, was visiting his parents. I'd seen him on several occasions in the building, and after Jeff died, we'd talk whenever he stayed with his parents. The last time he visited, we greeted each other warmly. He asked how I was. My answer was, "I'm okay." He responded, "But are you happy?" I hesitated momentarily and replied again, "I'm okay." I wasn't going to be inauthentic and provide a different answer. But I also understood why he was looking for a cheerier response from me. This kind young man simply wanted me to feel better and not be sad. I told him how much I appreciated his asking about me.

I'm grateful people care enough to ask about my well-being and want the best for me. Friends, family, and acquaintances may not always be able to put into words exactly what they wish to express, but I try to interpret their intention. More often than not, people are communicating a genuine sense of connection and concern. In those moments, it's not for me to correct them, but to give them the benefit of the doubt and accept their compassion as it was meant.

I'm much more aware of living in an appreciative state of mind and conscious of its power to uplift me. With this understanding, it's important to intentionally acknowledge the kindness of others and return those sentiments back into the world. Living fully in the small moments has much to offer when looking for renewed meaning in life. Feeling the grace of gratitude can be a compelling gift.

I Need a Sign

Rationality and irrationality live right next door to each other in your head. It's the consequence of pragmatic realities and the existential unknown confronting each other after a profound loss.

At some point, I knew I'd need to stop Jeff's cell phone service. He loved technology, especially his smartphone; he was attached to it as much as any 16-year-old. Jeff was also a prolific caller and often phoned me three to four times a day between seeing patients. He just wanted to say hi and tell me he loved me.

I delayed shutting off Jeff's phone service for a few months. Although meaningful calls had ceased within a month of his passing, I let the service continue. I told myself, you never know, he might have an account somewhere, like a streaming service or subscription requiring two-factor authentication, and I'd need his phone active to receive a text. But as the months passed, that issue didn't arise.

Finally, I set an arbitrary date to stop his cell service. When that day came, I became hysterical over this thought—how would he be able to call me if I shut off his cell phone service? This is not rational. All the same, I was distraught, feeling as though a vital piece of me was on the verge of being ripped away. Was I mourning, in the broader sense, that he and I would never again communicate in this mortal realm? Yes, I think so. But at that moment, it felt like I was severing our communication lifeline. My brain told me how irrational I was behaving, but my heart was being sledge-hammered inside my chest.

I had to wait a while the day I called AT&T until I could calm down and speak in sentences. I steeled myself, picked up the phone, and tapped in AT&T's number. You get transferred to a special department when you respond to the automated question, "How can we help you today?" and say you want to cancel your phone service. It's not a general call center, full of voices in the background trying to solve other customer's problems. You're transferred to an agent who specializes in discussing the reasons for your cancellation and handling the logistics of the process.

I ended up speaking to Sandra, a woman with a nondescript Midwestern accent. I told her I wished to cancel my husband's cell phone service and explained that he had passed away. Jeff and I bought new phones about six months before his death. We were on the three-year payment plan, so we still owed plenty of money on our phones. I thought I'd be stuck paying off his phone, or at the very least, have to return it to AT&T to cancel the loan. But AT&T did something unexpected. Sandra first offered her condolences, then said the loan would be canceled immediately, and I could keep the phone. That's AT&T's policy when someone dies.

Though I was relieved and grateful for this unexpected benevolence from a giant conglomerate, my sense of losing one more thing that signified Jeff was barely contained. I was so raw during that phone conversation, I did something I don't usually do. I told Sandra, a complete stranger, how hard it was to cancel my husband's phone service and why—that once I discontinued it, he could never call me again. My interior pain had scratched through to the surface, where it could be heard by a disembodied voice somewhere in America. I admitted I knew it sounded crazy. Undoubtedly, it had to be unsettling to hear. Having just shared an intimate piece of myself and my grief, anything could've come next as a response from this poor woman. It would've been completely understandable if Sandra had quickly moved on to finish our business. But, she didn't. Sandra

Adventure on Joyland Road

told me she understood and then shared her own experience of grieving for her mother. We talked a little longer, and she offered her condolences again before wishing me well. Sometimes, comfort can be found at unexpected times and in surprising places.

***

There are moments of despair when you look for a sign, anything that gives you the impetus to take another hopeful breath. Many of my signs seem to occur in nature. Somehow, I feel animals can take in the essence of a lost loved one. I know I'm not the first person to think this, but it's so irrational for me.

One summer morning, after an early outdoor swim, I spotted two Monarch butterflies alight on some flowers. It was a beautiful morning, and these two marvelous creatures were incredibly close to me. I approached cautiously, careful not to spook them. They seemed unbothered by my presence, continuing to linger over the rich nectar they had found. I had my iPhone with me and began taking photos. I wasn't quite getting the close-ups I wanted, so I inched forward. As I slowly approached, the butterflies didn't budge, they just seemed to pose. And then a thought flashed in my head: I felt so fortunate to get this close to these exquisite butterflies—it seemed providential—Jeff must be embodied in one of them. I began speaking softly to the closest butterfly, as if it were Jeff. *That's so completely irrational.* After about 10 minutes and 30 shots, they flew away. I take solace from those captured moments every time I look at the photos.

Lisa Rosenberg

I had the same experience when encountering a deer at the cemetery where Jeff is buried. I buried his ashes six months after he passed away. Because Jeff died so suddenly, during those six months, when his ashes were sitting on the sideboard in our home, I had time to figure out what would be the best way for me to part with him. But when I buried his ashes on that cold December day, I again experienced the trauma of his loss.

I visited the cemetery several times after the burial. One day, I was feeling especially down. As I drove to the section where his ashes are buried, I saw a large deer standing at his gravesite. I parked my car about 10 yards away and remained in the driver's seat. The deer picked up its head, looked at me for a while, and didn't move. I took photos again and sat there amazed. Eventually, the deer leisurely ambled toward a couple of its friends, but it didn't leave the vicinity as I slowly walked to the grave. The deer continued to munch on vegetation and occasionally looked in my direction. Once again, I perceived some divine intervention. It doesn't matter if I believed a fleeting essence of Jeff was embodied in that deer, or whether I created the thought from suggestible circumstances, as long as I felt the loss just a little less.

Whether you think a sign is divinely presented, or your mind is making connections to bring relief to your aching heart, I urge you to embrace it. Signs have more value than the immediate emotional comfort they provide. They also bolster your strength to take the next breath, walk out the front door, go on a vacation, or even sell your house and move to another state. Whatever gets you to take the next positive step in your life, trust your instincts.

The moral of the story is:
Take comfort and strength where you can find it.

Lisa Rosenberg

***

A few months after Jeff died, there was a day when I was on the verge of being inconsolable. There weren't any outward physical signs of Jeff's presence, and I badly needed one. And then it occurred to me—the sign I was looking for took place while Jeff was very much alive. It happened early in our relationship, the first night we spent together, when he said, "Don't worry, I'll take care of you." It's always stood out as the most incredibly romantic thing anyone has ever said to me.

In a parallel situation, there's a movie, Heaven Can Wait, with Warren Beaty and Julie Christie (a remake of Here Comes Mr. Jordan). It's one of my favorite movies for both its humor and sentiment. The last scenes in this movie weren't something I associated with Jeff when I first saw it, or the many times after, but I do now. In short, Warren Beatty's character dies prematurely but is allowed to temporarily return to Earth in another man's body. He finds the love of his life, but he and his co-star, Julie Christie, need to recognize each other after he must take on a different physical form. He tells her at two different points in the movie, "Don't worry, there's nothing to be afraid of." When he says that phrase in the movie's climax, she realizes this man she has never met before embodies the spirit of the person she fell in love with.

There are just some movies that resonate with you, and I've always loved this one because true love was able to overcome death. The transcendence of love means something different to me now. There's a sustenance it can provide when I'm so desperately in need of a sign.

The Legacy They Leave

When we intimately live in harmony with someone, respecting and admiring how they lived their life, it doesn't seem like a bad idea to blend the best parts of ourselves with theirs to evolve into better humans. Jeff will always be a part of me, and I must remember that. It just isn't easy sometimes.

When I talk about Jeff and share his stories, draw on his wisdom to counsel friends and family, or tackle a task around the house he used to do, I feel a deeper sense of him with me. I attempt to conjure up and internalize everything good, kind, and wise about him. When I can do that, I imagine the best of him is living on through me.

I tried to do just that when a family issue arose regarding Jeff's bar mitzvah prayer shawl, known in Hebrew as a tallit. The tallit has historically been worn by Jewish males though, in today's modern reformed Judaism, some women also wear a tallit in synagogue. The shawl is long and fringed, with a white background, generally blue or black stripes, and white fringes. The tallit, specifically the fringes, serve as a reminder of God's commandments, creating a closeness with God during prayer. Jeff's tallit had long been stored in a cranberry-colored velvet bag, adorned with a Star of David and Hebrew writing.

We kept the bag on a glass shelf in our living room for a long time, alongside my father's blue velvet tallit bag. It's customary for Jewish grooms to wear a tallit for their wedding nuptials. When our son got married, we brought the bag to his wedding so he could wear his father's tallit during the ceremony. Foolishly, neither Jeff nor I thought to take the tallit out of the bag beforehand to see its condition. As you might imagine, it was quite wrinkled. There was also a visible wine stain on the shawl's white background. Jeff's son took it in stride and wore his father's tallit proudly at his wedding. Right after the wedding, we had the tallit cleaned and pressed, but the stubborn wine stain remained. We had it cleaned again, but the dry cleaner explained the silk fabric was too old and delicate to work on any further. Ever the optimist in my skills, I gently tried to lighten the stain a touch more. I improved it slightly, but decided to quit while I was ahead.

    That took place over 20 years ago—fast forward to 2023. My granddaughter had her Bat Mitzvah in June. A couple of months before the event, my son asked for his father's tallit so he could wear it for the occasion. In September 2023, my California grandson, Brett, would celebrate his Bar Mitzvah, and I remembered Jeff's tallit would be worn by him as well. I figured I'd better start looking for it, which shouldn't have been too hard since we always kept it on a glass shelf in the living room. Except, it wasn't there. Jeff and I had remodeled our apartment the year before and packed up many of our belongings, which included everything in our living room. Is it possible I didn't put the bag back on the shelf in its rightful place? My father's tallit bag was exactly where it was before, why wasn't Jeff's?

    I know, I must've taken the tallit out of the bag and left it carefully folded over a hanger to keep it from getting wrinkled again. But it wasn't hanging in a closet, tucked into a drawer, or sitting on any shelf. I turned my house upside down three times, but the bag and the tallit were nowhere to be found. I was frantic. I couldn't ask Jeff what happened to his tallit, but he surely would've known.

    I gulped hard and texted my son, telling him I'd looked everywhere, but the tallit remained hidden. Hard on myself as usual, I felt utterly incompetent in that moment—like I was losing my mind. I then texted my daughter with essentially the same message. Right after I sent that message, she called me.

My daughter said, "Don't you remember, Dad sent me a box full of stuff about a year ago, and his tallit bag was in the box. Dad and I talked about Brett having the tallit for his Bar Mitzvah and keeping it. Didn't Dad talk about it with you?" As she continued to speak, I vaguely remembered we'd sent my daughter a box of items with some stuffed animals for her youngest child and other keepsakes. I didn't recall that one of the objects in the shipped box was Jeff's tallit. He also didn't discuss with me who would possess the tallit after he was gone. It probably didn't seem relevant to him at the time.

But it certainly became relevant, as both children wanted to "own" the tallit. My son made it clear to me, in no uncertain terms, that he wished to have the tallit. Mind you, Jeff didn't wear that tallit once during our 30 years together. He didn't pray in it or talk about it as an object that held deeply personal religious meaning. Yet, the children were attaching way more value to the tallit than their father ever did.

I was distraught at the thought of a bitter disagreement between Jen and her brother. I became uncontrollably weepy with my daughter at the possibility of a stand-off. "This is not what your father would've wanted. He wouldn't want you to argue about who should have his tallit. There are so many objects that will have to be divided between you two one day. This is just the first. Can't you both share the tallit for bar mitzvahs and weddings and then, one day, when we're all gone from this earth, it will be Brett's?"

Whatever goes on between siblings in all their moments of growing up together and then apart, often carries over into situations like this. Both children were emotionally invested in this object and seemed to be digging in their heels. I remained greatly troubled and wanted to "fix it," but the tallit had taken on a life of its own.

My son now knew the tallit had been sent to his sister. I didn't know how he would react to me, or more importantly, what he would think about his father. But my son didn't blame Jeff for the current state of affairs. He wondered if there might've been a misunderstanding between his father and his sister regarding how the tallit would be shared or kept. My son also said this wasn't my issue, it would be handled between him and Jen. I appreciated being sidelined on the matter; as much as I wanted to, I couldn't speak for Jeff and I didn't know his intention for the tallit. I surely know he never imagined this sort of fuss over it.

The tallit did find its way back to Chicago for my granddaughter's Bat Mitzvah, with my son respectfully wearing it for the occasion. The well-traveled tallit then flew back to California to make its next appearance on the shoulders of my grandson for his Bar Mitzvah. But that's not the end of the story. You see, that wine stain was still there.

A new tallit is one of the gifts the family often likes to give the Bar Mitzvah child when there isn't an heirloom tallit to hand down. And so it was for Brett. A family member wished to gift Brett a new tallit. But Jeff's tallit was already on hand, so a new one wouldn't be needed. But, somehow, the wine stain was innocently mentioned and became a point of contention. My son-in-law, Jonathon, a true mensch, was caught between the push and pull of a sentimental, stained tallit or the new one being proffered. He thought he had the perfect solution—remove the wine stain from the tallit, and it would be above reproach. Except that's not how it worked out. As I knew, the silk tallit was old and delicate, fragile from a long, earthly life. As Jonathon worked to remove the wine stain, the blue-dyed stripes ran into the white background of the tallit.

My daughter didn't know Jonathon had been trying to remove the stain, and when he told her what happened, she was upset and angry. He had done this to her father's tallit without her knowledge

Adventure on Joyland Road

or consent. Jonathon was beside himself with guilt over the outcome of his well-intentioned efforts. Emotions were running very high. I didn't know any of this until I innocently mentioned in a conversation with my daughter that a California family member had asked me about the wine stain. I wondered how they would know that. My daughter was deeply distressed as she shared the story with me.

I stayed composed as the story unfolded, and since Jeff's passing, I have come to understand my role in moments like this. Jeff isn't here to calm troubled waters or offer insights yet to be considered, but in these moments, I do my best to imagine what he would say. What can this situation teach us about how to move forward? What lessons does the tallit have to teach? I told my daughter the lesson for Jonathon is that he'll never be able to please everyone—in fact, when we try to do that, we often end up pleasing no one. For my daughter, the value of the tallit lies not in the tangible object itself, but in what it represents spiritually and personally. Whether worn for occasions or kept as a keepsake, its value rests in its sentimental significance and connection to the past. That's what her father would've wanted her to see. When I spoke to Jonathon a few days later, he apologized profusely. I told him I wasn't upset and repeated what I'd shared with his wife.

I spoke to Rabbi Dave, the generous and thoughtful man who officiated at Jeff's funeral and dedication, about the tallit and the meaning it held for the various people connected to its story. He said, "The tallit is the same. Nothing has changed. The religious significance of the fringes remains intact. The sentiment of the tallit hasn't changed either. It's still the tallit worn by Jeff at his Bar Mitzvah." As I told the kids, the value is in what the tallit represents, not what it looks like. The value is in the wisdom bound between the threads and the memory of the person who first wore it. The value of the tallit is in the lessons it has to teach.

But the story of the tallit was not quite over, though I thought it was. I was told Brett would wear a new tallit purchased for him by Jonathon's family. However, when I attended my grandson's Bar Mitzvah, Jeff's tallit made a surprise appearance—not in its physical presence, but its spiritual one. During a Bar or Bat Mitzvah ceremony, the parents of the child typically give a short speech, expressing their pride in their son or daughter and praising them for the hard work he or she has put into their religious studies. Jonathon was the one to deliver the following words:

> This is not the tallit that we originally intended to give you today. Your grandfather Jeff left you his tallit, and it was stained. I wanted your tallit to be perfect, so after consulting the internet (first mistake), I tried to clean it and inadvertently caused the colors to run. Needless to say, tie dye looks good on T-shirts but not on a tallit. I promise to you that I will get your grandfather's tallit restored, but in the meantime, we present you with this tallit.
>
> The author Voltaire wrote, "Perfect is the enemy of good." I think there's a really important lesson here. You strive for perfection, and you always have. There have been times when perfectionism has gotten you hamstrung and caused you to be reluctant to do things, especially things that look at the outset that they might be hard. Unfortunately, I think you get this trait from me. The painstaking research and study, whether it's deciding on a bass guitar or which tie to wear today, how to tie it, and whether you can pull off a pocket square with it (you look very sharp, by the way!). I'm guilty of going down rabbit holes too. Perfectionism has the potential to get in the way of enjoyment, experiences, and life. You are an exceptional person. I know many kids, and few have the self-discipline you have. This Bar Mitzvah is all you. There was no coercion necessary to get you ready for today. The same thing goes with your grades,

> music, and other passions. You don't need micromanaging which is incredibly rare in a tween.
>
> So back to the tallit: I felt horrible that I had damaged this family heirloom. Your Grandma Lisa did me a huge kindness and told me "Jeff was concerned with people and this was a thing and things can be replaced. While misguided, your intentions were good, and it's going to be okay." Hearing this lifted a huge weight off my shoulders. So, I'm going to pass that advice on to you. Take those risks, use that keen intellect, trust your values, follow that moral compass, and learn from your mistakes. Things will work out and Mama and I will always be proud of you. Oh, and I'll give you a freebie as you start this adventure into adulthood-don't wash this tallit!

I didn't know Jonathon was going to mention the tallit in his speech, and as it unfolded, my composure unraveled. Stunned surprise must have registered on my face, as I dabbed at the tears welling in my eyes. My niece, clearly affected by Jonathon's words, leaned over and asked if I had more Kleenex. First and foremost, through his speech, Jonathon brought Jeff's presence into the sanctuary. The speech was early in the ceremony, so my sense of Jeff being present and watching over us stayed with me throughout the service and the weekend.

I've since had many thoughts about Jonathon's speech. The lessons we hope to teach aren't always the ones heard, but that isn't ours to decide. Jonathon is a fine human being and was deeply mortified this mishap occurred with the tallit. He identified the important lesson, "perfect is the enemy of good," and expressed to his son that he may benefit from internalizing this life lesson early. (It's a lesson I could stand to hear again.) Jonathon also said he was determined to have the tallit restored. However, taking the philosophical and religious view, it isn't necessary to do anything more to repair the tallit.

The tallit's value, beauty, and wisdom are found in how it looks today. From the religious point of view, the purpose of the tallit, specifically the fringes, is to remind the wearer of the 613 sacred duties or commandments in the Torah. The shawl is simply the garment that serves to hold the fringes. From the personal and philosophical realm, this is the tallit my husband wore on his shoulders for his Bar Mitzvah in 1957. It has since come to take on a life and value beyond the tangible for all the lessons it can teach. The stain will always serve as a reminder, not of a mistake, but of all that can be learned from making a mistake. Imagine looking at this mishap and instead of saying, "I really messed up," one says, "This is the tallit Grandpa Jeff wore for his Bar Mitzvah. It's less than perfect but more precious for it."

As the tender, well-worn silk is felt between the fingers of his children and grandchildren, fond memories will drift back of their wise, funny, and loving Grandpa Jeff. The tangible object is more beautiful and has greater intrinsic value because, though battered and bruised, it is still here to tell its story. The layers of meaning and wisdom are revealed in the fullness of the tallit's exquisitely imperfect nature.

Reflections on Elisabeth Kübler-Ross and the Stages of Grief

I first read about the stages of grief as conceived by Dr. Kübler-Ross when I was in nursing school in the 1970s. I knew basically nothing about dying or grief. The only experiences I had with death as a child were when my grandparents passed away. My father's mother, Lillian, lived in our home until I was 10. She was like a companion to me when I was a child. Lillian would watch me play when I was young and, in her strong Eastern European accent, gently admonish me not to jump on the furniture, as I was prone to do. My grandmother was also diabetic. I remember sitting with her every morning as she gave herself insulin injections. Perhaps that early exposure to chronic illness treatment fueled my interest in a healthcare career.

Early one morning my grandmother suffered a stroke. An ambulance arrived, and the paramedics carried her down from her second-floor bedroom on a stretcher. She was taken to the hospital and died shortly thereafter. I wasn't allowed to go to the funeral. I remember feeling quite upset I was the only one in the household who wouldn't be attending. My two older sisters were going to the funeral, so a sitter stayed with me. My mother gave me some rationale that a funeral wasn't something for a child to attend. I disagreed, but to no avail.

When my family returned home, I was eager to understand

what had transpired. Even now, 60 years later, I can still recall my mother telling me how my Aunt Mary tried to throw herself onto the casket, reinforcing the idea that tragic events like this unleashed terrible, uncontrollable emotions. It was best I hadn't been there to witness such sights. The message was clear: experiencing the death of a loved one and the grief that followed was something to be avoided.

Then I encountered the seminal work of Kübler-Ross as a young nursing student. Grief was a subject to be discussed openly, and if you had ever loved someone—or were going to love someone—it was inevitable. There were stages: denial, anger, depression, bargaining, and acceptance. At the time, this framework for understanding the grieving process was taught in a linear fashion; these were the stages people go through consecutively when they suffer the loss of a loved one. You experience all the stages and eventually come out the other side. Kübler-Ross later wrote she didn't intend for the model to be interpreted and taught this way. She, and her co-author over the years, David Kessler, tried to dispel the idea of a linear, undeviating progression through all the stages. The grieving process is, in fact, non-linear. People can go back and forth among stages, remain in one for a while, or perhaps not experience every stage.

And now I'm here 50 years later, amid grief I never could've imagined, thinking about Kübler-Ross. The depth and complexity of this process are stunning and bewildering. When I reflect on my own experience with the stages of grief, I realize I have not been big on experiencing anger—I simply haven't. A friend assumed I must've been angry at the doctor for not being more perceptive or paying greater attention to Jeff's clinical picture the month before he died. I tried to explain why I wasn't angry: it just didn't seem productive. She replied, "That's so you." We always bring our baseline selves into the grief process. Though I was quick to anger in my younger years, as I've aged, I try to be more solution-oriented when problems arise.

Adventure on Joyland Road

You can't think straight if you're angry—save your outrage for when it counts. Jeff was, in large part, responsible for teaching me that. I also realized that letting anger take hold would keep me trapped, deplete my energy, and impede my path forward.

Kübler-Ross and Kessler's book, *On Grief and Grieving*, is an excellent resource, one with detailed information on various aspects of the grief process. Perhaps more importantly, it allows the reader to feel they are not alone, and that the depth and intensity of their grief and despair are shared by many.

In 2022, Carlsson offered an updated perspective on the grieving process, presenting more current views on how it is experienced. Instead of viewing grief as moving in a step-like fashion from anguish to "recovery," the grieving process is more of a fluctuation between engaging in working through one's grief and needing to take a break from it. The idea of having to let go of your loved one has changed to "maintaining a healthy bond to the deceased." Carlsson doesn't believe the stage theory of grief can capture the complexity of how people grieve. The interplay of emotional, spiritual, physical, social, and practical needs is multilayered and individual to each bereaved person. More recent perspectives on grief see it as a process in which the loss has disrupted an important aspect of a person's sense of meaning in life and must be "reconstructed."

Bereavement is, indeed, incredibly complicated as it affects every aspect of one's internal and external life. "Maintaining a healthy bond to the deceased" is a particularly important concept and a key part of understanding what it means to move forward in a positive and productive way. And, the reconstruction of one's purpose and meaning in life plays a starring role in the grieving process. Determining the meaning of one's life is a basic existential question. Why should you push on and keep moving forward every day?

I believe that, for the aggrieved, there isn't a "better" way for a loved one to die—whether expected or sudden, there is no get-out-of-grief-free card. My scorched soul is no more or less deserving of sympathy than anyone else's who has lost their loved one in a different way. Each survivor's path shares many commonalities with others who grieve, but each also carries their own distinct distress and suffering, shaped by the very nature of how the death occurred—the sights, sounds, and smells—none of which can be erased from memory.

That said, I was curious about what researchers had to say about losing a loved one suddenly—especially when the survivor was present and had tried in vain to save their life, as I did. In 2022, Carlsson studied the phenomenon of unexpected loss, looking at the lived experience of bereaved family members losing a close person following death by sudden cardiac arrest. When the deceased has an illness or condition known prior to their death, those close to that person generally have a chance to prepare. For those who lose a loved one suddenly, there is no chance to prepare, as they are placed in the situation involuntarily. The experience of sudden loss is associated with a higher mortality rate.

Other studies that interviewed survivors suggest there is added trauma and stress for family members if they witness the cardiac arrest at home, and then are present during resuscitation efforts. Posttraumatic stress and other psychological reactions are not uncommon when these situations occur. If a family member is initially providing life-saving support and is unsuccessful, the trauma is only magnified. The experience of sudden loss and its surrounding circumstances can sometimes make it harder to move forward in the grieving process, impacting the bereaved person's health and well-being.

In their 2014 guide to treating traumatic bereavement, Pearlman and his co-authors discuss several factors that distinguish a sudden death from an on-time death—that is, one that's expected. They believe the psychological consequences after a sudden, traumatic death are markedly different from those of an expected death. The

Adventure on Joyland Road

survivors of a sudden death usually experience all of the sadness and anguish associated with grief, as well as other signs of trauma. Many survivors develop symptoms of posttraumatic stress disorder (PTSD). "Survivors of traumatic death must contend with a number of additional issues that are difficult and painful." The authors suggest that because there was no chance to prepare or say goodbye, the death may be much harder to accept. It can be difficult for the survivor to make sense of or find meaning in the deceased's death. Loved ones may become preoccupied with issues of blame, guilt, and responsibility. It's common for survivors to be concerned about whether their loved one suffered in their last moments. And fundamentally, any assumption that one can "predict or control" what happens in this world is shattered, triggering a sense of exposure and vulnerability.

When I reviewed the material above as a mental health professional, I took note of the specific issues and risks to the survivor's future physical and mental well-being, particularly the need to look for signs and symptoms of PTSD. As the real survivor of the sudden loss of my husband and best friend, the phrase "So, Mrs. Lincoln, how was the play?" comes to mind. The clinical research I've read on grief and mourning affirms some notions I had already intuited—such as the loss of meaning and control, and the shifting of one's identity after the death of a spouse. Yet, I am mostly left feeling numb and parched. While research like this and the National Institute of Health document, *Bereavement: Reactions, Consequences and Care*, can inform us about correlations among variables and offer theories on the concepts that underlie survivor narratives, it doesn't satisfy the yearning to have the true depth of surviving a loved one's death revealed.

The timing of when you read any book or article about death or grieving can affect you emotionally in different ways. One night, perhaps six to eight weeks after Jeff died, I picked up *The Year of*

Magical Thinking by Joan Didion. She's a wonderful, internationally acclaimed author who I greatly admire. Didion lost her husband, John, to a sudden cardiac event that occurred in their living room while they were having dinner. The very first words of her book, chapter 1:

> *Life changes fast*
> *Life changes in the instant*
> *You sit down to dinner and life as you know it ends*
> *The question of self-pity.*

Her words ripped through me. I could feel my face tightening, but I soldiered on thinking that diving into someone else's grief might somehow help me.

Grief when it comes, is nothing we expect it to be . . . Grief is different. Grief has no distance. Grief comes in waves, paroxysms, sudden apprehensions that weaken the knees and blind the eyes and obliterate the dailiness of life.

A few pages later, Didion describes how those who have recently lost someone often feel invisible, except to other survivors who recognize the stark, exposed look on their faces. They too have seen that look when they gazed in the mirror and saw the reflection of their own grief. They recognize the cloud lingering within and the invisible shadow it casts. This perception is tangible for those who have grieved deeply, but it remains imperceptible to many, leaving one suspended between two realms of existence—being seen and unseen.

Joan Didion is killing me as I sit reading her words in my living room. She gets it—really gets it—but it's too soon for me to read this book at night, alone, with this exquisite author giving voice to thoughts that slash at my already wounded heart. I started skimming the pages to get to the end of the book, but it left its mark on me for a few days. Someone had lyrically captured moments of my grief while I was experiencing them in full force. I didn't understand the impact it would have on me that night. I wasn't ready.

Several months after Jeff died, I read a few chapters in Kübler-Ross and Kessler's book. They allowed me to feel confirmed—that I was experiencing thoughts and emotions shared by many grieving people. At other times, the content was too much for me, and I felt overwhelmed and distressed. I have subsequently read many other authors who have scientifically or personally written about death, bereavement, and the experience of loss. There are threads of validation and pearls of wisdom to be gleaned, nodding to the fact that what I'm feeling, thinking, and living through is not new but has been experienced by millions of others. It is the human condition.

Irvin Yalom is noteworthy for his profound and personal encounter with grief. He's a man I greatly respect and have read throughout my life. Dr. Yalom has had an illustrious career. He is a board-certified physician in psychiatry and neurology, spending almost his entire professional life at the Stanford University School of Medicine as a clinician, teacher, and researcher. He's written 23 books, both fiction and nonfiction, had movies made from his books, and written more articles and book chapters than can be recounted here. In his autobiographical notes, Yalom says, "Psychiatry proved (and proves to this day) endlessly intriguing, and I have approached all of my patients with a sense of wonderment at the story that will unfold. I believe that a different therapy must be constructed for each patient because each has a unique story." Irvin Yalom's clinical skill in psychiatry is equally matched by his ability to write about those stories. He has brilliantly explored many aspects of the human condition and has extensive experience working with the dying and their loved ones.

And yet, when faced with the death of his beloved wife, Marilyn, and the aftermath of "deep, shattering grief," a lifetime spent exploring, investigating, and writing about the experiences of grief—as well as providing therapy to the dying and bereaved—did not prepare him for the soul-searing pain of her death from multiple myeloma. His book, *A Matter of Death and Life,* which he and Marilyn co-wrote as she was dying, is an intimate portrait of how each approached her looming, inevitable death. Yalom is unflinchingly self-reflective and possesses a remarkable capacity to describe his state of being. He articulates his "deep abyss of grief but how could it have been otherwise . . . even now, as I think how blessed I was to have spent my life with you (Marilyn), I can't understand how it all happened." He speaks of the "soothing of magical thinking" and even describes the crushing blow of selling his wife's car after her death, just as I described selling Jeff's. How completely un-ironic. When you've lost your beloved, all the small moments of grief share a stunning commonality with those of other survivors. No two humans are the same, yet we are bound by connections that run deep, often unseen and unspoken.

 A few months after Marilyn died, Irv, as he refers to himself throughout the book, reflected on a book he'd written many years before, *Momma and the Meaning of Life.* The specific chapter was "Seven Advanced Lessons on the Therapy of Grief." He discusses a patient, Irene, who saw him for unresolved bereavement issues. Irene sought Dr. Yalom's help because she felt he was "the only person smart enough to treat her." Yet, Irene seemed resistant to developing a therapeutic alliance with Dr. Yalom. She had suffered two significant losses in her life—her husband's and her brother's deaths—and would tell Dr. Yalom that, in his snug and secure life, still surrounded by family and loved ones, he couldn't possibly understand the nature of what had been lost. "You can't imagine, nothing bad has ever happened to you," Irene says. "What can you really know about loss. Do you think you would handle it any better?" Both the patient and therapist verbally wrestled with each other but remained engaged in the therapeutic process. After three years of therapy, Irene made progress and ultimately remarried.

Dr. Yalom reflects on his encounter with Irene and acknowledges that, in hindsight, she was right—he couldn't understand then what he has come to know now. If he had, he would've been a better therapist. If he were to see Irene today, he feels their work together wouldn't play out the same way; he would "experience her differently" and find "a more genuine and helpful way to be with her."

I read *A Matter of Life and Death* after I'd written a great deal of this book. I don't believe I could've gotten through the book in the early months after Jeff passed away. I ached reading how deeply Irvin Yalom was affected by the death of his wife, this man I greatly respect for his skill in psychiatry. Instead of looking through a keyhole, he humbly opened a door for me, revealing a room not filled with scientific observations and analytic thinking, but with a man in full—standing there, broken into pieces, just as I was. I can't exactly say there was comfort in that, but I did feel less alone, realizing no amount of intelligence, insight, or experience can truly prepare you for losing your treasured love.

I wish I'd read some of this material before Jeff died, as a kind of anticipatory guidebook. But why would I have? I didn't expect what was to come, nor would I have wanted to entertain the thought. And there's no way to prepare or steel yourself for how this level of grief affects you, or how you'll move through the process. I wish I could tell you otherwise.

And while taking a cavernous dive into what's written on dealing with the loss of a loved one, existential questions arise. These questions recur and appear without notice, seeming to have a life of their own. How will I find renewed meaning in my life? Will anyone ever love me again unconditionally? Will my loved one be waiting for me when I die? Answers to some of these questions will reveal themselves over time, patience is required. Other questions have no definitive answers, at least in this lifetime, and one must find a way to make peace with that.

"I want to engage in the eternal conversations with the ancestors and sages. Despite it all, I want to live my life in praise and awe—in wonder and hope. Even if I am wrong. Even if at the end there is nothing but darkness."
Rabbi Will Berkovitz

Wait for Me

I had the good fortune of being invited to Door County, Wisconsin by my neighbors for a long weekend. It's a four-hour trip from the northern suburbs of Chicago and another invited neighbor, who happens to be a widow, offered to drive. There was plenty of time to talk, and Sarah and I were chatting non-stop the whole ride up and back. Sarah had worked in public education before she retired, loves to travel, and shares my enjoyment of the wonders of nature. She's an excellent traveling companion and a lovely human to spend time with.

Sarah is also a woman of great faith. She's Catholic, attends church most every Sunday, and is involved in many charitable endeavors. She often wears a cross around her neck, her devotion easily displayed. She said her husband was also strong in his religious beliefs, and they shared their devoutness throughout the marriage.

With a perspective markedly different than mine, I thought Sarah might be a good person to ask about her thoughts on an afterlife. Sarah didn't hesitate to respond, saying she believes in a celestial life beyond this one. She trusts she'll be reunited with her husband when she dies. After Sarah shared her candid and deeply held conviction, she looked at me and said, "Don't you?" For a moment, I was at a loss for words. I said I wished I had her deep belief—it would make the rest of my existence on this earth easier to bear. I envy the comfort that must come from faith and the belief in a life with your beloved after this earthly one.

Before Jeff died, I didn't think much about what occurs after you die. We were together in the here and now, and I was grateful for our relationship every day. Why spend time looking over the precipice? With no religious training in my formative years and no spiritual inclination to plumb the depths of my future existence in another realm, I never felt motivated in my adult life to bring my thoughts to that space. That lack of spiritual introspection persisted throughout my marriage to Jeff, as he showed little curiosity about spirituality or what it meant to no longer exist.

Though Jeff went to Hebrew school and had a Bar Mitzvah, he wasn't interested in continuing his religious studies once that ceremonial event occurred. Jeff told a story about his lack of desire for any further religious education after his Bar Mitzvah. The synagogue where he attended Hebrew school was considered conservative. The Conservative movement falls between Orthodox and Reform Judaism in terms of how observant a person is of historical religious traditions and beliefs. For example, does the person keep kosher, do they consistently observe the Sabbath? After Jeff's Bar Mitzvah ceremony, there was a luncheon for the guests. The Rabbi purposefully approached Jeff and his parents and said, "I assume Jeff will be continuing his post-Bar Mitzvah studies with me at the synagogue." Jeff didn't give his parents a chance to respond. He promptly answered, and I'm paraphrasing, that once he left the synagogue, he would keep walking and not return.

I don't think the Rabbi took this comment well, particularly from a thirteen-year-old. That statement would come back to haunt Jeff four years later, during the last semester of his senior year in high school. Every Friday afternoon, senior students in his high school in Monticello were required to go to their synagogue, church, or temple and spend the afternoon with the rabbi, priest, reverend, monk, or designated religious teacher in that place of worship. Apparently, in the early 1960s, you could still mix religious and secular education and get away with it. I have no idea what they did with a kid and their family who declared themselves atheists.

Dutifully, Jeff did as he was told and showed up at the synagogue of the rabbi who officiated his Bar Mitzvah. Other students from his senior class were also in attendance. The rabbi began his teachings, and during this first afternoon, he pointedly asked Jeff a question requiring religious knowledge. When Jeff was unable to respond correctly, the Rabbi said, "Well, if you had attended post-Bar Mitzvah studies, you'd know the answer."

The following Monday, Jeff met with the teacher responsible for arranging the Friday afternoon sessions. He told the teacher he would not be returning to his synagogue for the rest of the term, and they'd need to let him stay at school during those periods. The teacher was taken aback and said that wasn't possible, there was no one available to supervise Jeff. Jeff reiterated he wasn't going back to the synagogue every Friday afternoon—essentially, to be humiliated. The teacher became flustered and continued to repeat himself, as did a resolute Jeff. Finally, Jeff said he'd leave school at noon on Fridays and go home for the rest of the day. Not exactly a compromise, but the teacher relented. Jeff was a top student in high school, already accepted into a good four-year college. He was also a formidable opponent, even as a teen, so the teacher just let it go.

The cautionary tale here is that forcing religious conviction or using ridicule to make someone engage meaningfully with their faith isn't a strategy built for success. People need to find, through some level of introspection, why religion or a belief in God is important to them.

Despite the lack of formal Judaism Jeff and I incorporated into our adult lives, we strongly identified with being culturally Jewish. There isn't a definitive definition of being "culturally Jewish," but it's an amalgam of habits, beliefs, and a way of perceiving the world—similar to what any other culture would consider characteristics shared by those who identify as part of their group. For example, both my father and Jeff's father understood and spoke Yiddish. Yiddish was, and still is, a language spoken by central and eastern European Jews (Ashkenazi). It incorporates a good deal of the German language, Hebrew, and words from other modern languages. It was a "secret language" used by my parents when they didn't want me or my sisters to know what they were saying. It may not be the best way to teach or pass down what is now a less-spoken language in Jewish Ashkenazic households, but like Jeff, I picked up several words and phrases along the way. I still sprinkle them into my conversations with both Jews and non-Jews. Several Yiddish words have made their way into the American vocabulary, such as klutz (clumsy person), nosh (snack), and schmooze (friendly chat). Jeff and I also shared a very similar sense of humor—the secret sauce of our marriage—which was shaped by being raised in Jewish households and the prevalence of Jewish comedians during our formative years.

Now that Jeff isn't here, I've had more encounters with my faith. Profound grief has propelled me to travel down roads previously unexplored. Inexplicably, at least at the time, I felt strongly compelled to have a rabbi officiate Jeff's funeral service. When Jeff's ashes were buried and lowered into the small grave in the national cemetery, I wanted the rabbi to say Kaddish on that cold and sleeting day. When we dedicated Jeff's headstone, I wanted the rabbi to be there to consecrate the ceremony. Religion and spirituality had never been important to me, yet here I was, taking every step I could to make it part of the process.

I light Yahrzeit memorial candles on every appropriate occasion to honor Jeff's memory. Besides on the anniversary of his death, as configured to the Jewish calendar, one can light a memorial candle on Yom Kippur, the Jewish day of atonement and fasting. The candle is lit because there is a thought in Jewish tradition that "a person's soul and essence are like a candle in the world." When lighting the candle, one can reflect on the unique illumination the person being remembered brought into the world and intentionally shepherd that into one's heart. As I considered how to become a better human being on that holy day, remembering Jeff in this purposeful way felt right.

I've also begun attending some of the Jewish high holiday services with family and friends. At times, I've streamed them by myself. Some of the prayer book passages are quite beautiful, and I find comfort in them. As I can't read Hebrew, I greatly appreciate how every Reform prayer book provides a transliteration to English. An especially poignant passage during the Rosh Hashanah service was based on Deuteronomy 1:6-7 called *You Have Stayed . . . Go Forward*:

> *You have stayed long enough in this place, God said.*
> *Time to go forward.*
> *Turn your face to the future.*
> *Believe that you can cross this sea and survive.*
> *Inside you is a Moses; within you Miriam dances, unafraid.*
> *Lift up your voice and sing a new song.*

These are inspirational words, ones you can reflect on when trying to be more self-forgiving and finding your way down a new path.

On one Yom Kippur, I attended morning and afternoon services with my neighbors. They belong to a local congregation, but we streamed the services in her apartment because she was on crutches from a knee injury. The night before, I lit a memorial candle for Jeff. It was a beautiful day that Monday, so between the morning and afternoon services, I walked to Jeff's grave. The last hour of the afternoon service was particularly meaningful to me. It's called Yizkor, a public observance for bereaved congregants. Yizkor means "to remember." Though the remembrance is part of a traditional public service, the recollections are an inward memorializing. I found this service deeply moving, and the passages recited from the prayer book resonated with me.

That night I had many dreams. For my entire life, I've been a person who's usually had "bad" dreams. Mostly, they're anxious dreams, like being late for an exam or failing to find the room where it's being held. On occasion, these dreams—really nightmares—are scarier, and I wake up screaming. Rarely were my dreams of a pleasant nature or ones where I was completely in control, mastering a challenge, or defeating an attacker. Jeff would say that most dreams were residue from the day—unresolved issues your unconscious was working through as you slept. When I'd tell Jeff my unsettling dreams, his first question was, "What do you think they mean?"

Maddening!

"Why do you think I'm asking you? You're the psychiatrist!" I'd respond in exasperation.

But he persisted and made me tell him what I thought the dreams meant. It's what a good psychiatrist does.

When I fell asleep that night after the Yom Kippur services, I had several anxious, unsettling dreams. In one particular dream, everything was falling apart in a house where I was living. I woke up and started to think about what these dreams were related to from the day. I didn't get very far before I fell back asleep. Then I had an incredibly unusual dream for me. I dreamt that Jeff was with me in the house from my earlier dreams, but none of what had been going wrong mattered anymore. We were lying on the floor talking, embracing, kissing. We were becoming passionate. I said in the dream, "I know you're gone, but I feel you here with me." Dreams often have a fragmented, two-dimensional, black-and-white feel. This dream was vivid and in living color—it fully engaged my senses. I could feel Jeff's presence both physically and emotionally. It's one of the very few times I've felt Jeff come alive so completely and intensely since he died.

And so, Jeff would ask, "What do you think those dreams mean? What are they related to?" The first dream of a house in disrepair represents my grief process—my internal disarray, emotional upheaval, and the many ways it's affected me. I believe the second dream is related to the meaning of the Yizkor service. There was a reference in the service to the light and goodness of the departed loved one continuing to live inside you. I've often told myself that very thing since Jeff passed away. Sometimes it rings hollow, other times, it seems as true as I know the sun rises and sets. In that dream, I believe his presence resonated into every synapse of my unconscious mind, bringing comfort through his memory, even as I grieved his loss. When I awoke shortly after, I was nothing short of astonished at having had such a dream. I was even more amazed at how peaceful I felt, as if some wispy strand of Jeff's essence had buried itself deep within me, bringing a sense of calm.

My connection to the readings, the services, and the sense of community found in houses of worship are, I suppose, my attempts to make sense of Jeff's sudden death—to find, if not answers, then comfort in the spiritual. All my understanding of psychological processes and the wisdom I've gathered over decades of living still offer little discernment into the unknowable.

Before I fall asleep, I often say, "Jeff, if it's possible, please wait for me" (I hope he feels the same). I fervently wish that Jeff and I could be together in whatever comes next. That thought gives me a moment of hope. Yet, I remain a realist without the comfort of a long-established belief system offering such benevolence—I simply don't know. I remind myself that my only choice is to live my best life here on earth: do good, stay connected with family and friends, and make Jeff proud. It's what gets me out of bed every morning. Still, with every fiber of my being, I hope he's there waiting for me when I take my last breath.

This Is Not Creepy

While some people are still alive and breathing, they think about what inscription they might like on their headstones. I gave no thought to this before Jeff died; it seemed kind of morose. When he passed and I had to create the inscription for his headstone (three lines, with a maximum of 15 characters per line), I gave some serious thought to what I might want to have written on mine.

My ashes will be buried in the same plot as my husband's—we'll share the same headstone, his inscription on the front and mine on the back. That's how couples are buried in national cemeteries these days. Rather than have my family struggle and be challenged by the task of writing a headstone inscription for me, I've written my own. Part of my core identity is to be a teacher. I'm going to use my headstone to convey the best life advice I can give in 45 characters. These words aren't going to make me immortal, but I'm okay if they are my legacy.

Love deeply,
laugh, be kind,
have purpose.

Loving others deeply is what you do with body and soul; it is all-encompassing. It's why we are here.

Laughter is what keeps your brain from being fried to a crisp by the insanity that surrounds us.

Kindness is what your heart is made for.

Adventure on Joyland Road

Having purpose is in your bones—it keeps you moving through good times and bad, until you can move no more.

Adventure on Joyland Road

Looking back on what I've written, I realized I wasn't just writing my thoughts on grieving after a sudden loss—I was writing a love letter to my husband. Writing about him was a celebration of his life as an everyday hero. There are so many extraordinary people we've lost from our lives who were everyday heroes—good, compassionate people who took care of their families and chose to put others before themselves. They did it quietly, without expectation of accolades. My Jeff loved telling stories from his life. No better way to end than to share his favorite.

Jeff told many stories about things that happened to him during his early life growing up in Monticello, New York, but the story he most often shared was his adventure on Joyland Road. Jeff was a teenager in the 1950s, and at that time, Monticello was still a resort destination in the Catskills. Before the widespread use of air conditioning and jetting off for summer vacations in the U.S. and beyond, Jewish New Yorkers would flock to upstate New York for the cooler weather and the abundance of activities these Catskill resorts offered. Resorts named Kutsher's, the Concord, Grossinger's, the Nevele, Laurels, the Flagler, Schenk's, and many more were part of the Borscht Belt, just a 90-minute drive from New York City. Three full meals a day, group activities, sports, shopping, spas, and top-notch night-time entertainment kept visitors busy all summer.

The pastoral towns where the resorts were located swelled from a few thousand inhabitants to over a million people in the summer.

Adventure on Joyland Road

However, the only way the year-round inhabitants of the towns visited the resorts was as employees. Though the 1950s and early '60s were the heyday for the Borscht Belt resorts, these towns were still largely rural, populated by farmers, merchants, and tradespeople. And in and around those small towns were many backroads for adventurous teens to explore.

It was 1962, the summer before Jeff and his friends, Sam, Steve, and Ira, would go off to college. Jeff was heading to Union College in Schenectady, NY, Sam and Ira to SUNY Buffalo, and Steve to NYU. For these young men, it was a big move from small-town life and from families where boys like Jeff and his friends were the first to attend college. One afternoon Jeff decided they should take a ride in his dad's Cadillac and explore some of the country roads around Monticello. Taking your bike was one way to explore, but when you're 17 years old and with your best friends, nothing beats taking your dad's Cadillac for a spin. Fatefully, they ended up on Joyland Road. When you're about to enter exciting, uncharted territory in your life, how could you not be curious about what lies at the end of Joyland Road?

The boys hadn't explored this road before, apparently too far even for a long bike ride. What started as a smooth paved road, gradually became a charming gravel rural road, which soon narrowed into a gravel path—growing more pitted, constricted, and sandy as they boldly forged ahead. Large trees on either side grew closer to the road, their overhanging branches blocking the full illumination of daylight. Ever the intrepid explorers, the boys ventured on quickly and fearlessly. It was the quick and fearless part that kept Jeff from noticing the railroad ties directly in front of him. As the Cadillac went airborne and panic surged through Jeff's veins, the car quickly found its resting place—a golf course sand trap.

The boys jumped out of the vehicle to assess the situation. They might all have been smart enough to get into college, but getting a

Cadillac out of a sand trap was entirely another matter. But soon enough, they weren't alone. A groundskeeper must've heard the commotion and came running over. He was as alarmed as the boys. The groundskeeper quickly told Jeff to get back in the car, shift into neutral, and steer while he and the other boys tried to push the car out. After a bit of maneuvering and lots of heavy muscle work, they managed to push the car out of the sand trap. Jeff got out of the car to thank the groundskeeper and offer some way to repay his kindness, but the groundskeeper waved him off, saying, "Look, kid, just get out of here!" The boys jumped back in the car and took off.

There was no outward damage to the Cadillac—apparently, cars were built like tanks in those days. Jeff returned it to his dad that afternoon hoping the car's adventure would remain untold. And for two weeks, nothing happened. Then one day, his father said, "Jeff, I noticed a lot of sand on the floorboard of the car." Without hesitating, Jeff replied, "You know, Dad, a lot of these backroads get pretty sandy." And his dad said nothing more. But Jeff knew his dad had somehow found out what happened that day. This was his subtle way of letting him know.

Jeff always marveled at how if the events of Joyland Road happened today, there would be criminal charges, fines, damages to pay, and who knows what other consequences. As Jeff reflected on his adventure over the years, he'd say, "You know, you could never get away with something like that these days. Times have changed."

Like the Borscht Belt that disappeared long ago and the teen adventures occasionally revisited like well-worn passages from a favorite book, as you say goodbye to one era of your life and step into the next unknown journey—indeed, times do change.

Epilogue

I didn't realize until deep into writing this book just how significant some of the stories were. At first, I took Joyland Road at face value; it's a charming story from my husband's past that he loved to tell. But I found this story has a more significant lesson hidden within it. That's why recounting our stories is so important, for in them lies the guidance we desperately seek.

Joyland Road lives beyond the events that occurred that day in 1962. Indeed, times do change. We wind up in situations we never imagined. We hurtle forward in this life hoping for the best, but misfortune and hardship are inevitable. We struggle and persevere, and incredibly, our friends, family, and sometimes even strangers are there to pull us out and help us get back on the road. You may not know what lies ahead, no one does. From there, the only choice is to keep putting one foot in front of the other, savor the small moments, and—as Jeff said—keep moving forward.

Lisa Rosenberg

Quintessentially Us

Notes

Aristotle. (2009). *Nicomachean ethics* (W. D. Ross, Trans.). The University of Chicago Press. (Original work published ca. 350 BCE)

Berkovitz, W. (October 3, 2014). *Forgiving God on Yom Kippur* (Commentary). Religion News Service. https://religionnews.com/2014/10/03/forgiving-god-yom-kippur-commentary/

Bisaz R., Travaglia A., & Alberini C.M. (2014). The neurobiological bases of memory formation: from physiological conditions to psychopathology. *Psychopathology*. 2014;47(6):347-56. DOI: 10.1159/000363702

Bragg, R. (1997). *All over but the shoutin'*. Vintage Books.

Britannica. *Yizkor*. https://www.britannica.com/topic/yizkor

Carlsson, N., Bremer, A., Alvariza, A., Arestedt, K., & Axelsson, L. (2022). Losing a close person following death by sudden cardiac arrest: Bereaved family members' lived experiences. *Death Studies*. Vol. 46(5), p.1139-1148. https://pubmed.ncbi.nlm.nih.gov/32755272/

Didion, J. (2005). *The year of magical thinking*. Vintage Books.

Elfers, J., Hlava, P., Sharpe, F., & Arreguin, S. (2023). Resilience and loss: The correlation of grief and gratitude. *International Journal of Applied Positive Psychology*. DOI:10.1007/s41042-023-00126-1

Emmons, R. A., Froh, J., & Rose, R. (2019). Gratitude. In M. W. Gallagher & S. J. Lopez (Eds.), *Positive psychological assessment: A handbook of models and measures* (2nd ed., pp. 317–332). American Psychological Association. https://doi.org/10.1037/0000138-020

Gawande, A. (2014). *Being mortal*. Metropolitan Books.

Institute of Medicine (US) Committee for the Study of Health Consequences of the Stress of Bereavement. *Bereavement: Reactions, Consequences, and Care*. (1984). Osterweis M., Solomon F., & Green M., (Eds.). Washington, D.C.: National Academies Press (US). https://www.ncbi.nlm.nih.gov/books/NBK217842/

Kessler, D. (2019). *Finding meaning*. Scribner.

Kiken, L.G., Lundberg, K.B., & Fredrickson, B.L. (2017). Being present and enjoying it: Dispositional mindfulness and savoring the moment are distinct, interactive predictors of positive emotions and psychological health. *Mindfulness*. Vol. 8. p.1280–1290. http://doi.org/10.1007/s12671-017-0704-3

Kübler-Ross, E. & Kessler, D. (2005). *On grief and grieving*. Scribner.

Leder, S. (2021). *The beauty of what remains*. Avery.

Lewis, C.S. (1961). *A grief observed*. HarperCollins.

Miller, M. *Remembering the Borscht Belt*. Aish. https://aish.com/remembering-the-borscht-belt/

Neimeyer, R. A., & Sands, D. C. (2011). Meaning reconstruction in bereavement: From principles to practice. In R. A. Neimeyer, D. L. Harris, H. R. Winokuer, & G. F. Thornton (Eds.), *Grief and bereavement in contemporary society: Bridging research and practice* (pp. 9–22). Routledge/Taylor & Francis Group. https://doi.org/10.4324/9780203840863

Pearlman, L.A., Wortman, C.B., Feuer, C.A., Farber. C.H., & Rando, T.A. (2014). *Website supplement for treating Traumatic bereavement: A practitioner's guide*. The Guilford Press. http://efaidnbmnnnibpcajpcglclefindmkaj/https://www.guilford.com/add/pearlman/appx_hands.pdf?t=1

Rosenberg, L. (1991). A qualitative investigation of the use of humor by emergency personnel as a strategy for coping with stress. *Journal of Emergency Nursing, 17*(4), 197-203.

Rosenberg, L. (1995). Sick, black and gallows humor or are we having any fun yet? In *Nursing perspectives on humor.* Buxman, K. & LeMoine, A. (Eds.). Power Publications.

Shiva: The resource for Jewish mourning. *What is Shiva?* https://www.shiva.com/learning-center/understanding/shiva.

The Statue of Liberty–Ellis Island Foundation. *Ellis Island.* https://www.statueofliberty.org/ellis-island/overview-history/

Valikhani, A., Ahmadnia, F., Karimi, A. & Mills, P.J. (2019). The relationship between dispositional gratitude and quality of life: The mediating role of perceived stress and mental health. *Personality and Individual Differences.* Volume 141, 2019, p. 40-46. https://doi.org/10.1016/j.paid.2018.12.014

Van Manen, M. (1997). *Researching lived experience.* Althouse Press.

Waldinger, R. & Shulz, M. (2023). *The good life,* Simon & Schuster.

Yalom, I. (1980). *Existential psychotherapy.* Basic Books.

Yalom, I. (1999). *Momma and the meaning of life.* Harper Perennial Modern Classics.

Yalom, I. (2015). *Creatures of a day.* Basic Books.

Yalom, I. (2021). *A matter of death and life.* Redwood Press.

Yalom, I. https://www.yalom.com/biography.

Acknowledgments

I'm deeply grateful to my family and friends, who lifted me up and helped carry me through a sea of grief. You never left my side and still haven't. You helped me understand the many ways love exists in this world. I would name you all, but you appear in the stories I tell, and I want to maintain your privacy. I hope I have told you enough how much you all mean to me.

Along the way, some of my friends read drafts of this book. You encouraged me there was value in my words; it gave me the strength to keep going. Thank you for that gift.

Cyril Mukalel and the Potter's Wheel publishing team have been a godsend. Trying to get a book commercially published can be a soul-crushing experience. Cyril read my work and saw its potential to help others. Thank you so very much, Cyril, for believing in me.

www.ingramcontent.com/pod-product-compliance
Lightning Source LLC
LaVergne TN
LVHW051824080426
835512LV00018B/2717